Do you sometimes feel that you are wandering in a wilderness of grief, confusion, faltering faith? If so, you are not alone. Like the lost children of Israel many have searched for a way through a personal wilderness. But just as those same Israelites followed God's leading to the Promised Land, you too can find the promised new life in the Spirit.

Jamie Buckingham made such a journey — not only figuratively but literally. During a time of devastating personal experience he traveled to the Sinai. There he found restoration and, in the solitude of a wilderness night, he learned ancient Bible truths that would alter his life forever.

Now he shares with you the simple, healing secrets that God first revealed to Moses at the dawn of faith.

A WAY THROUGH THE WILDERNESS

JAMIE BUCKINGHAM

Chosen Books

A Division of Baker Book House
Grand Rapids, Michigan 49506

Library of Congress Cataloging in Publication Data

Buckingham, Jamie
    A way through the wilderness
      1. Christian life—1960——   2. Moses (biblical
leader)   I. Title
BV 4501.2.B827   1983   248.4   83-7371
ISBN 0-8007-9093-6

A Chosen Book
Copyright © 1986 by Jamie Buckingham
Chosen Books are published by Fleming H. Revell
a division of Baker Book House Company
P.O. Box 6287, Grand Rapids, Michigan 49516-6287

ISBN: 0-8007-9093-6

Fifth printing, October 1992

Printed in the United States of America

Dedicated to
all God's children
who are walking through
a dry and barren wilderness

"See, I am doing a new thing!
Now it springs up; do you not perceive it?
I am making a way in the desert
and streams in the wasteland."

(Isaiah 43:19, NIV)

In Appreciation:

My fellow sojourners who across the years have followed me on pilgrimages through the Sinai.

1976
Bruce Buckingham
Randy Ostrander

1978
Dallas Albritton
Bob Crumley
Derrel Emmerson
Mike Evans
Gib Jones
Bill Nelson
Angus Sargeant, M.D.**
George Sowerby
Hugh Welchel
Frank Whigham
Bob Wright
John Zentmeyer**

1979
Dick Blackwell
Dick Bolen
Wayne Buck
Stan Elrod***
Mickey Evans**
Jim Gills, M.D.
Charles Kopp
Dick Love
Willie Malone
Peter Marshall
Francis Nicholson
Angus Sargeant, M.D.**
John Sherrill
Steve Strang
John Zentmeyer**

1980
Mel Anderson
Steve Anderson
Jim Bauman
Gene Berrey
Stan Elrod***
Zane Elrod
Bill Ilnisky
Mike Karl
Joe Ed McGahey
Richard Payne
Alton Reeder, M.D.
Carl Wills
Cecil Wilson

1982
Peter Darg
Stan Elrod***
Mickey Evans**
Rick Foster
John French
David Hinders
Leonard LeSourd
Derald McDaniel
John Tripp
Jack Wells, M.D.

Guides
Ora Lipschitz
Norman Lytle
Shai Sofer
Amir Azia
Timi ben Yoseph

**Two-time sojourner
***Three-time sojourner

Contents

Introduction

In the Footsteps of Moses

Few places on earth are as remote, yet as evocative, as the "great and terrible wilderness" of the Sinai. The very name stirs childhood memories of stories emanating from that awesome and holy place.

Each time I have been there, though, trekking the burning sands and climbing the craggy mountains, I have become even more aware of the eternal nature of God. In this place are still found the principles that enable all God's children to make it through their own personal wildernesses.

The conflicts faced by those early Israelites—about 3,200 years ago, as they left Egypt for the freedom of a promised land—still beset us all. Fear. Uncertainty. Grief. Anger. Doubt. Discouragement. Temptation. These are the constant companions of all pilgrims. Those wandering ancients faced them all.

But though the problems linger with us, the solutions are equally apparent. I found my answers not only as I sojourned through the Sinai but as I struggled through my own personal wilderness.

Some years ago, as I emerged from the dark night of my own soul, when it seemed I had not only destroyed myself and my family but done damage to the Kingdom of God by my foolish actions, I determined to trace the physical path of those early searchers of promise. My first trip to the Sinai was a terrifying experience. I spent the entire two weeks trying to adjust to the shock of desert living. But I was fascinated by the place and returned again and again.

During those subsequent trips, I discovered there is indeed a way through the wilderness. The path has been clearly marked by those who have gone before. Any man or woman who dares turn his back on whatever holds him in bondage can still find the Promised Land. The principles of deliverance are the same today as they were when Moses led the Exodus 3,200 years ago.

I stood on the banks of the *Yam-Suph*, the Sea of Reeds (mistakenly translated as the Red Sea, which I will explain later), marveling at the grace of God that opened the water before the children of Israel. I suffered from drinking the bitter waters at Marah, rested in the wonderful shade at Elim, climbed Mt. Tahuneh where Aaron and Hur held up the hands of Moses, and I stood on the summit of *Jebel Musa*—the Mountain of God—where God thundered His law and covenants for all history to hear and heed. I hungered at the Graves of Craving, wept in the awesome stillness of the desert nights, and laughed with my companions as we discovered hope and joy in unexpected places. In the end, I climbed Mt. Nebo and viewed, as did dying Moses, the lush green of the Promised Land on the other side of Jordan.

Through all this burning wilderness I found evidence of the presence of God. No longer does He traverse the desert in a pillar of cloud by day and a column of fire by night; instead He speaks in the still, small voice heard by Elijah in this same place. Thus the wilderness remains a place of purification and preparation—a place where a man can learn to distinguish between the clamoring voices of this world and the often quiet, gentle voice of God.

From the dawn of civilization the Sinai has been a place of conflict. This seemingly worthless piece of gritty land—looking on the map like a sharp wedge driven between Africa and Arab Asia—has been the most besieged territory in the world. At last count it had been the battleground for at least fifty invading armies since the time of recorded history. As a result, it has been occupied by some alien force ever since the Early

Bronze Age—five thousand years ago. It remains today as it was in the time of Moses, a giant and scorching crucible that has melted armies, destroyed kings, and burned from proud men both sin and selfishness until they have emerged pure and prepared for ministry.

The Sinai peninsula is an arid wilderness of mystic and *Geography* ethereal beauty. Dunes and marshes line its northern coast along the Mediterranean Sea. A limestone plateau, called *el Thei*, with low hills ending in a sharp precipice that stretches nearly the entire width of the peninsula, fills the central portion of the triangle. It barely supports enough vegetation to feed the goats and sheep of the ever-wandering Bedouin tribes. In the south, rugged mountains lie between the Gulfs of Suez and Aqaba, forming rows of granite walls that change color with each passing hour.

Caravans of merchants have traversed the *Via Maris*—the "way of the sea"—along the Mediterranean to the north, bringing their wares across the golden crescent from Africa to Asia. This was known also as "the way of the Philistines" and has remained, to this day, a place where wars have been fought.

In the south, where the high mountains jut upward from the desert floor, divided only by the mysterious wadis or dried waterways that separate them, Moses first met God at a burning bush. He later returned with the entire nation of Israel as they fled from the bondage of Egypt and stopped at this same mountain to hear the thundering voice of God give the Ten Commandments, which have formed the basis of all law in the Western world.

Moses' journey began on the banks of the Nile in Egypt and ended on the lonely peak of Mt. Nebo in Jordan. On the map, the distance between these two places is not much greater than that between New York City and Washington, D.C. But the geography is dwarfed by the scope of events that took place here. It is, as another pilgrim once remarked, an exceedingly finite place for the infinite to have happened.

Most scholars say it was during the time of Rameses II, who reigned from 1304 to 1237 B.C., that the Exodus took place. Central to the story is a man called Moses. No man in history towers taller. Called *Moshe* in Hebrew, *Mosa* or *Musa* in Arabic, and *Moses* in English (by way of the Greek), his footsteps still go before all who walk through their own personal wilderness—making their way from the bondage of sin and traditionalism to the liberty and freedom offered by God.

Though the infant Moses was pulled from the bulrushes along the Nile by the daughter of Pharaoh, Moses likely kept in contact with his Hebrew family while growing up. His mother nursed him as a child, and two older siblings—Aaron and Miriam—would have been his early playmates. The Israelites had earlier—perhaps as much as 400 years earlier—migrated to Egypt from Canaan. Their champion in Egypt was the next-to-youngest child of Jacob, Joseph, who had been sold into slavery by his jealous brothers. Joseph had risen to second-in-command in Egypt and found a place of refuge for his family when they appeared needing food. In subsequent years, however, *"there arose up a new king over Egypt, which knew not Joseph,"* and Goshen, where the Israelites lived, became a house of bondage and slavery. For almost ten generations these once-proud people were slaves to the Egyptians, building their pyramids and making bricks for their houses.

Although Moses was raised in the palace of the Pharaoh, he never lost contact with his roots. The day came when he could no longer take the hypocrisy of pretending to be one man while really being another. Angered beyond control at the injustice being done his people, he killed one of the Egyptian overseers whom he had seen beating an Israelite slave. When his crime was discovered, this prince of Egypt was forced to flee into that void of wind, sand and rock shimmering in a blue haze to the east—the wilderness of Sinai.

Over the next forty years Moses went through a gradual transformation. He met and married a Bedouin shepherd girl, Zipporah, and moved in with her family headed by the Midianite priest, Jethro. In essence, he became a Bedouin shepherd, wandering with the other nomads tending sheep and goats. In this atmosphere he raised his two sons, Gershom and Eliezer. Also in this atmosphere he had deeply impressed upon his mind that there was but a single God, rather than the many gods worshiped in Egypt. Even though he had doubtless heard the story of the God with no name and no image from his own people in Egypt—a story that had been passed down by word of mouth around the late-night campfires—it was from Jethro, a distant relative of Abraham, that the concept became reality.

At the end of this forty-year period, Moses, now 80 years of age, heard a voice from God while tending Jethro's flocks near the base of Mt. Sinai. As far as we know, it was the first time in 400 years that the Lord had confronted one of His chosen people. Nor had any man ever been summoned to a more important task. "I am sending you to Pharaoh to bring my people the Israelites out of Egypt" (Exodus 3:10).

Thus, out of the burning desert emerged not a prince of Egypt but a prophet, returning to lead his people into a land unknown to any of them but promised of God. Reinforced with signs and miracles and awed by the determination of the man he had sent into exile so many years before, Pharaoh finally succumbed to the pressures of God. The children of Israel were released to find their way through the wilderness to the land of promise.

What follows is history: the opening of the sea to allow the Israelites to pass through, the miracle of water from the desert, manna every morning, and finally a great military victory on the eve of hearing God's voice from Mt. Sinai.

At Rephidim the Israelites were attacked by a desert people called the Amalekites. Moses climbed nearby Mt. Tahuneh with his brother Aaron and his brother-in-law Hur. As long as Moses stretched out his wooden staff over the valley below, the troops, under Joshua, advanced. When his arms grew tired and fell, the Amalekites advanced. To assure victory, Aaron and Hur had to hold up Moses' arms.

I climbed that mountain early one morning. At the urging of my friends, I stretched out my arm over the imposing valley below as the imaginary legions of Amalekites advanced and receded in my mind. After five minutes my arm and shoulder ached so much my arm began to drop. Two friends, laughing and calling me a poor leader, stepped in to hold up my drooping arm. Even then, as the heat of the day drained my energy, I realized I was no match for the man of God who had once stood at this same place interceding for his people. The cost of apostleship, I saw, was much greater than the accompanying glory.

Down the wadi from Rephidim the land opens into a great plain called *er Raha*, where the children of Israel encamped at the base of the Mountain of God. There, rising into the rich blue sky, is the magnificent three-columned granite apex of Mt. Sinai. Mt. Sinai is actually a massif of several mountains. The highest peak is *Jebel Katerina*, 8,651 feet, touched by *Ras Safsafa* and *Jebel Musa* (the Mountain of Moses), which soars to the height of 7,497 feet.

It is impossible to approach Mt. Sinai—much less climb to its awesome summit—without being overwhelmed by the glory and majesty of the huge mass of granite and gneiss rock. It glows a deep purple in the sunset and flashes red and gold in the light of dawn. When the noonday sun beats mercilessly on its barren sides, it turns almost white. Even when snow covers its peak in the winter, the awesomeness of its craggy nature still thunders from beneath the blanket of whiteness. It is one of the world's truly unique places. It was here that the entire mountain range thundered and quaked as God spoke to His people; and regardless of the fact that there are no holy places, only holy people, this place still bears, indelibly, the footprint of God.

From Mt. Sinai Moses turned north—an eleven-day journey—to the oasis of Kadesh-Barnea near the border of Canaan. But the Israelites balked at entering the Promised Land. As a result the entire nation was condemned to wander in the wilderness until a new generation whose moral fiber was uncorroded by slavery grew up to possess the land promised by God. Therefore, even though he had already spent forty years in the Sinai, Moses was forced to spend another forty years until this grumbling nation of Israelites was ready to follow God's command.

Somewhere near Kadesh-Barnea occurred the pivotal incident in the life of the old leader. In a final test, God asked him to speak to a rock and bring forth water. Instead, Moses reverted to a technique he had used many years before—and hit the rock with his staff. The toll of the wilderness had been too much. Bound by tradition, he was unable to obey. As a result, while Moses stayed behind on the lofty peak of Mt. Nebo, the new generation of Israelites finally crossed into the Promised Land under their new leader, Joshua.

According to an old Jewish tradition, God kissed His faithful servant as he died. And in the book of Jude, we read that while Satan contended for Moses' body, God sent the archangel Michael to stand guard. Deuteronomy records that the aged prophet was buried by God Himself and that *"no man knoweth of his sepulchre."*

The wilderness does not have to be a place of hopeless fear and utter despair. Despite the hard lessons learned, the taste of bitter water, the conflict with self, nature and desert enemies, it can be a place of tranquil beauty, perfect rest and warm fellowship with fellow pilgrims. To bypass the wilderness in our journey to the Promised Land is to bypass God. And what is the use of occupying a land of promise unless the God of promise goes with us?

In eulogizing the Irish poet William Butler Yeats, who often wrote from his own desert place, W. H. Auden wrote a poem that ends:

> Follow, poet, follow right
> To the bottom of the night,
> With your unconstraining voice
> Still persuade us to rejoice . . .
> In the deserts of the heart
> Let the healing fountain start.
> In the prison of his days
> Teach the free man how to praise.

This is the purpose of the wilderness experiences of life—to lead us to the place where the healing fountain starts.

Prologue

There is an ancient legend of an old Bedouin sheikh—the priestly patriarch or chief elder—of the Jebeliya tribe. His name was Sheikh Awad, and he lived in the high mountain region near the base of Mt. Sinai.

Early morning of the day he was to be officially set apart as the sheikh, an angel visited him.

"As the spiritual leader of this tribe of wandering nomads," the angel said, "you will need special wisdom."

The old man knelt in the sand and held his hands up in acknowledgment of his need.

"God is going to give you a special gift of discerning truth," the angel continued.

Suddenly the angel was gone. But when the wizened old man opened his hand, there was a small round stone in the palm—left, no doubt, by the angel. The stone had special mystical qualities that enabled the sheikh, when sitting in judgment over his people, always to know if a person was lying or telling the truth.

When Sheikh Awad died, his son inherited his father's position of spiritual leader of the Jebeliya tribe. He also inherited the stone, which he then had set in a ring.

At the tribal councils, which were held at the tomb of Sheikh Awad, the stone was always used to discern the truth. If a man was accused of lying, the Council of Elders would call all the men of the tribe together. The stone, now set in the ring, would be placed in a glass of water. After the man testified, he would be required to drink of the glass three times. If he had lied, he would drop dead.

The elders often pointed to the many graves around the tomb of Sheikh Awad as solemn testimony of the ring's power.

One afternoon a small group of us paused at the tomb of Sheikh Awad on our journey inland across the wilderness toward Mt. Sinai. Entering the nearby *maqad*—the single-room stone shelter next to the whitewashed tomb—we sat on the sand floor as our guide told us, again, the story of Sheikh Awad and his mystical stone.

"Last year," our guide said, "I was here when the Council of Elders held court. For the first time I saw the stone. It is now in the belonging of the son of the son of Sheikh Awad."

He then related a fascinating story. A Bedouin man had been robbed of certain goods that he later found in the tent of another man. The accused man denied he had stolen the goods, saying he had bought them from a third man. The third man, however, when questioned, denied ever having had the goods.

Someone was lying.

The Council of Elders called the men of the tribe together. More than 600 men came on camels and by foot, gathering at the tomb of Sheikh Awad—where we were at that moment.

The son of the son of Sheikh Awad called the two accused men forward. Again both denied guilt. The sheikh then brought forth the ring and the glass of water. He dropped the ring into the glass and handed it to the first accused.

The man took three quick drinks—and with a smile turned and handed it to the second accused.

The man stood, staring into the glass. Then, without drinking, he handed the glass back to the son of the son of Sheikh Awad.

A great cry went up from all the men standing around the *maqad*. Guilt had been determined and the elders quickly ruled a fine plus return of the stolen goods. The mystical gift from the angel had once again distinguished between truth and error.

When I began research on this book, I too asked for the gift of Sheikh Awad. I did not expect, nor desire, a stone. I asked for something far more meaningful to me—the internal gift of the Holy Spirit to enable me to discern truth from error and the ability to communicate that truth to my fellow pilgrims struggling through the wilderness places of life.

It is difficult, in the Sinai, to distinguish between legend and fact. How many Israelites made this journey? Did they travel through the deep wadis of the south, or across the sand by the Way of the Philistines to the north? Did Moses really strike a rock and bring forth water? And which mountain is really the mysterious Mt. Sinai—the Mountain of God?

Even though I have opinions, I have left the eternal debates of questions to scholars. For truth—the truth I wish to communicate in this book—is not relegated to historical places or even limited to whose interpretation of Scripture we accept. It is found, rather, in the still small voice that speaks to the hearts of men.

So, despite the diversities of opinion that surround the epic events of the Exodus, there are principles found in the Bible that, if applied to whatever wilderness you are passing through, will lead you from bondage to freedom, from darkness to light, out of the wilderness into God's land of eternal promise. For in its pages we will meet that perfect Guide who still says, "I am making a way in the desert."

What I share in this book is truth, the kind of truth that will set you free. Having said that, I do not hesitate to drink from the glass.

Jamie Buckingham
Melbourne, Florida

A WAY THROUGH THE WILDERNESS

I

Hospitality

"And where is he?" [Jethro] asked his daughters. "Why did you leave him? Invite him to have something to eat."

(Exodus 2:20)

The first reaction to any wilderness is withdrawal. The pain of losing a loved one, the shock of losing a job, the deep disappointment of being betrayed by someone you love—all tend to drive us into deep withdrawal.

Invariably our first reaction is, "Leave me alone."

God understands this. He also understands our even greater need to be part of a family—to be touched by loving hands, held by loving arms. Thus, into every wilderness experience of ours, God sends special messengers to minister to us. To Jesus He sent angels. To Elijah He sent ravens. To Moses He sent an old Bedouin sheikh.

Jethro, with warm, simple hospitality, helped the former prince of Egypt emerge from his shell of grief and self-pity and enter a world of preparation, a world designed by God to train him for the time he would return to Egypt for a far greater purpose.

Moses, at age 40, had been second-in-command in the most powerful and academically advanced nation of history. As an infant, he had been rescued from the sword of Pharaoh and raised by Pharaoh's daughter as a prince. Trained in courtly manners and given the best education available, his foster mother looked for the day when Moses would replace her father on the throne of Egypt.

But God had other plans, plans that could come to pass only after the egotism of Egypt had been burned from His servant in the crucible of the wilderness.

It began, as most wilderness wanderings begin, with an act of sin. In the Egyptian province of Goshen, where the Hebrew slaves were toiling in the blistering sun making bricks in the stiff clay pits, Moses killed an Egyptian taskmaster who was whipping a defenseless Hebrew slave.

It was a chivalrous act, well-meant, springing largely from human sympathy. Ironically, it was one of the first genuinely unselfish things Moses had done. At the same time, it was an act of murder, and the consequences were swift and merciless.

In his own strength, Moses was not strong enough to lead. So, using the justice of the Egyptians, God did something that still mystifies mortal man: He began the process of spiritual education by thrusting Moses into the great and terrible wilderness of the Sinai. Here he learned to distinguish between passion and principle, between impulse and settled purpose. Only in the wilderness does one learn that mere need never constitutes a call. One learns to wait on the voice of God.

Formal education is only the beginning of spiritual preparation. At the age of 40, Moses entered God's graduate school. The next forty years were spent in the deprivation of the wilderness. These were years in which his rough edges were sanded smooth. The literal blast furnace of the Sinai refined the character of a man God was going to use. There he learned to pray and he learned the values of solitude. There, starting with a few sheep and goats, he learned the principles of leadership. But he did not have to struggle alone. God put a family around him—the family of Jethro—who taught him the ways of the desert people, the ways of hospitality.

Moses had been into the Sinai before, but always as a military commander, never as a solitary pilgrim. There is evidence he may have led at least one expedition as far south as Dophkah, where the remains of an ancient Egyptian temple still stand at the site of the turquoise mines near Serabit el Khadim. But viewing the desert from a pharaoh's chariot is much different from viewing it as a lonely sojourner in exile, plodding through the sand and clambering over the rocks: a man who had lost not only his country but his family as well.

Filled with despair and confusion, the once prince of Egypt staggered into the burning crucible of the wilderness.

Making his way across the peninsula to nowhere, he began his wanderings. Awed by the blood-red sky at dawn, the star-studded cover of the night canopy, by the gaunt face of a primeval crag, by the vast emptiness, by the seemingly end-less stretch of burning sand, he stumbled on until he came to an oasis. Exhausted, he drank from the pool of water, then fell into the shade and slept. He was awakened by human voices speaking the ancient language still spoken by the old Israel-ites in the slave quarters of Egypt.

Young maidens, Bedouin girls in their early and mid-teens, had come to water their father's flocks. Shepherds from other tribes were at the oasis also. Recognizing the girls as strangers in the area, they were driving them away. Still angry from everything that had happened to him, Moses emerged from the shadows to strike out at the shepherd bullies. His wooden staff swinging, he charged at them, prepared to do to them what he had done to the Egyptian taskmaster. They fled, and the shepherd girls, grateful, once again drove their flocks to the water at the pool.

Giggling and hiding behind their veils, they returned to the nearby tent of their father, the Bedouin sheikh called Jethro (also called Reuel) who had moved his tribe from the territory southeast of Aqaba to forage in the Sinai.

"Why did you leave him?" Jethro quizzed his daughters. "Invite him to have something to eat."

That night Moses sat in the tent of Jethro and ate his first wilderness meal. He was about to learn the first of many wilderness lessons.

Sitting in the tiny *succoth,* or thatched hut made of date palm leaves, Moses watched, fascinated, as Jethro's beautiful young daughter Zipporah ground grain brought with them from Midian. Two large round stones were placed on top of each other. The bottom stone had a small trough around the edge. The top stone had a wooden handle affixed to one side so it could be turned on an axle that joined both stones in the middle. The maiden slowly poured the grain through a hole in the top stone, at the same time turning the stone so that the grain was crushed between the stones. The flour was collected in the small trough at the edge.

When there was enough, Zipporah added water and salt to the flour, kneaded it into a dough ball about the size of a grapefruit, then patted it out into large flat cakes about an inch thick. Next Zipporah laid the cake—called *libre**—directly onto the glowing coals made from dried camel dung. Watching carefully to see it did not char, she then flipped it over so the baked side was on top. Scraping up sand and ashes, she covered the entire cake, coals and all.

In a few moments her mother arrived with a huge dish of boiled mutton and herbs that had been cooking in another booth. Zipporah then brushed the sand from the bread and, holding it between her hands, slapped it with both hands in a clapping motion, knocking off sand and char.

Jethro motioned for the family to be seated, crosslegged in a circle around the fire. Moses sat next to the sheikh as the honored guest. Before eating they prayed. It was a strange experience for Moses. There were no images, no idols, just the mention of an unknown God, "El."

"Who is this El?" Moses asked. "Is He like the sun god *Re*, the river god *Osiris*, or *Hathor* whom the Egyptians worship at Dophkah?"

"I have heard of these false gods," Jethro replied, tearing off a piece of bread and dipping it into the stew bowl. "El is higher than them all. There are no gods but Him. El is at the center of all being. He spoke in times past to our father Abraham. Your ancestor Jacob bought a parcel of land for one hundred pieces of silver at Shechem in Canaan and set up an altar to El, whom he called *El Elohe* or *El Elyon*, the Most High God."

"I have heard that story from my mother in Egypt, but none of my people know the name of that god. It has long been forgotten. They know Him only as the god with no name and no image—the god of Abraham, Isaac and Jacob."

Jethro smiled and nodded. "I, too, am a son of Abraham. My ancestor, Midian—the fourth son of Abraham by Mother

* This same bread, when cooked on a piece of metal laid over the coals, is called *fatir*. It is similar to the modern pita bread of the Middle East, though it is thinner and does not have a double crust, or pocket. It is often cooked over dried camel dung, small pellets about the size of charcoal briquets, which burn like charcoal.

Keturah—was sent away into the east country. Our people tell of a visit by El to Father Abraham when he was one hundred less one. El changed his name from Abram, exalted father, to Abraham, father of many. Abraham then called El by the name of *El Shaddai*—God Almighty. He and all the males in his household were circumcised as a sign of the covenant that is yet to be fulfilled."

Moses sat long into the night, listening to the fascinating stories of Jethro. It is easy to learn from a man of hospitality.

This unwritten code of hospitality is still practiced in the Sinai. It is a code that originated with Abraham, whom Jew and Moslem both call "Father of Hospitality." It was Abraham who first decreed that the essentials of life were never to be denied any wilderness pilgrim, be he friend or enemy.

In Genesis 18, Abraham was approached by three strangers as he camped at Mamre. Sitting at the entrance to his tent, the childless, discouraged old nomad, the first of the Bedouins, saw the men approaching across the desert. He quickly brought them water to drink, then provided the extra luxury of water to wash their feet. Finally he offered them the shade of his tree.

The tree, mentioned in Genesis 18:4 and later in verse 8, is known as an *eshel*, or tamarisk, tree. After the wayfarers had eaten and been refreshed, they blessed Abraham by announcing Sarah would have a child. The Jewish Talmud says Abraham then responded by saying, "Now bless him of whose bounty ye have eaten. Think not it is of mine ye have eaten. No, it is of Him who spoke and the world was created."

One of the old Talmudic sages explains that *eshel* actually means a hospice, and consists of the initial letters of the three words that indicated hospitality: *achila* (food), *shetiya* (drink) and *lina* (accommodation for the night).

After the treaty with Abimelech, the Philistine chieftain, Abraham planted a tamarisk *(eshel)* tree in Beersheba (Genesis 21:33) to remind all who passed that way of the bond of hospitality among desert people. Ever since, the wells, the fire and the shade have belonged to all mankind.

There is no greater pleasure for the Bedouin than that of offering hospitality. Welcoming travelers is at the core of desert culture and is performed even if it means sharing the last piece of bread.

One evening just at dusk, our small group of desert travelers pulled into a Bedouin camp that consisted of two tents and an old tin and cardboard shack. We had been traveling all day through the narrow wadis and across the burning sand trying to reach the Gulf of Suez in our two Land Rovers. At that point we hoped to pick up the path traveled by Moses, which would lead us eventually to Mt. Sinai itself.

As the sun settled in the west, we noticed black clouds building to the south over the high mountains. Gusts of wind brought the smell of rain. We had been sleeping out each night, spreading our sleeping bags under the stars since it seldom rains in the desert, nor is there any moisture from dew. Thus we had no shelter in case it did rain during the night.

As we drove into the Bedouin camp, the old patriarch came out of one of the tents to greet us. Instead of asking, "Where are you from?" or even, "What do you want?", he grinned, extended his hand to all and welcomed our group of twelve men with *"Ahlan Wa Sahlan"*—"You are part of the family."

That night we had no choice but to sleep in his tent. He insisted. It would have been a great insult to have refused him the privilege of giving us the finest he had to offer. In return, he and his family crowded into the tiny cardboard and tin shack. Fortunately it did not rain, for they would have been soaked. Yet it would have made no difference to them. To have entertained strangers was the highest honor that could have come their way. Although we were welcome to stay the accepted three and a half days, we left the next morning, our hearts warmed, our stomachs full of their food.

Every passerby is invited to stay and relax. He is then offered little cups of strong, bitter coffee—the Bedouin equivalent of a cocktail. He may also be handed a steaming hot glass of extra sweet tea, prized by the Bedouin as a source of quick energy. Honored guests are feted with the meat of a goat slaughtered especially for them. To the Bedouin, whose entire wealth is in his flock, this is indeed a sacrifice.

So strong is the code of hospitality that rejection of it is received as an insult. A Bedouin demonstrates his kindness by sharing the little he has. A well-known story tells of a Bedouin who slaughtered his famous stallion, the fastest horse in the desert, in order to serve his guests a meal. He preferred to part with his beloved mount rather than risk being called a miser who did not show proper hospitality.

Likewise, the tent of the Bedouin is looked upon as a place of refuge. The host, once he has accepted a guest, feels obligated to protect him at all costs—even at his own peril.

During the Turkish rule of the Sinai, two fugitives once took refuge in the tent of a great Bedouin sheikh just as they were about to be caught by pursuing soldiers. When the soldiers arrived, they demanded the chief hand over the culprits. The old chief, standing before his tent with rifle in hand, refused. One of the soldiers decided to enter the tent and arrest the wanted men. Instantly the Bedouin raised his rifle and fired a deafening shot. The soldiers turned back, only to discover the chief had not shot at them; he had shot and killed his favorite mare.

"Be careful," an old man standing near the tent said to the soldiers. "The chief has just killed what is most dear to his heart. He has nothing more to lose."

The Turkish soldiers understood and fled back into the desert.

It was this lesson of hospitality Moses learned from Jethro— the first of many lessons he was to learn from this wise old sheikh whom God had sent into his life as a professor of postgraduate studies.

I, too, have encountered such hospitality at the hands of the Bedouin. Late one afternoon, as the sun was sinking in the west, my Jewish guide and I were invited into the tent of an old Bedouin sheikh whom I had met on a previous journey into the Sinai. He insisted we join him for coffee and then stay for dinner, such as it was.

We protested, not wanting to impose on his meager supply of food. He grinned a toothless smile and said he had no choice but to be our host. Waving toward the darkening sky, he reminded us of an old Bedouin proverb: "As long as the evening star shines, I am bound by Allah to offer hospitality to my guests."

We entered his tent while his wife scampered off to fix a few things for supper. Motioning us to sit, he busied himself with a brass *finjan*, an ornate, narrow-necked coffeepot blackened on the bottom from years of use over an open fire. He introduced us to his family who joined us, sitting crosslegged on the sand in a semicircle around the small fire that burned in the entrance to his tent. While I tried to converse with our host in my broken Arabic, my guide pointed to my hat. I thought he was telling me I should remove it as a courtesy to the Bedouin tent. But when I took it off, my guide took it from me, rose and disappeared outside the tent.

A few minutes later he returned. My hat was filled with small round camel droppings. The guide, realizing that the old Bedouin was making coffee and would need more fuel, had gone outside and picked up a hatful of dried camel dung to be used as we might use charcoal for a fire. When our host saw the expression on my face—after all, it was my hat filled with camel dung!—he laughed so hard tears rolled down his wrinkled brown cheeks.

I eventually joined in the laughter, but only after thoroughly beating my hat on the ground to remove any trace of its recent cargo.

I watched as our host, clad in his *galabiya* (a sort of caftan), his head covered with a checkered *kafeyah*, mixed the ground coffee with a generous measure of cardamom seeds called *hell* in Arabic. Adding water, he placed the *finjan* directly on the glowing coals of the dung fire, which filled the tent with pleasant, spicy smoke. He then joined us in the circle, sitting crosslegged with his robe draped over his spread knees.

When the coffee began to bubble and steam, he reached down with his bare hands and lifted the brass *finjan* off the fire. Ceremoniously he poured coffee into tiny glass cups which were brown-stained inside from many such occasions. I glanced at my guide and he nodded discreetly. Custom demanded I drink it. Despite the filth in the bottom of the glass cups, I smiled at my host—and sipped. It was so bitter I had to work to keep from sputtering. But I drank it all. Slowly.

While all this was going on, a young Bedouin man, obviously a member of the household but without the open friendliness of the old sheikh, entered the tent. Seeing us, he stiffened. Without speaking or acknowledging our presence in any way, he quickly took a seat on the ground outside the circle near the back flap of the tent. Only after remaining there several minutes, listening intently to our conversation, did he finally join the circle. Smiling, nodding politely, he poured himself a cup of coffee from the pot which had been replaced on the coals, and later he joined us in the dinner of pita bread, goat's cheese and fried chickpeas that had been mashed into a paste to go on the bread.

Later my Jewish guide explained the Bedouin custom. The young man, he said, was examining us to determine if we were friend or enemy. Thus he did not join us in the circle to begin with but sat at the rear of the tent until it became clear to him we were trustworthy. Had he gotten up and left without joining the circle, that would have been a sign to the sheikh that we were not to be trusted—even though the hospitality code demanded we be fed just the same.

A similar procedure is used if a member of the tribe brings a guest to the guest tent or hut. If he sits down beside his guest, it is a sign the man is a friend. If he ushers the guest into the inner circle, however, and then sits down next to the wall of the tent, apart from his guest, it is a sign he has been coerced into bringing the guest. Even though the man is welcomed and fed, he is still suspect. One of the men in the tent will always keep his hand on the handle of his dagger, just in case the wolf sheds his sheepskin before the meal is over.

All this is done to preserve hospitality, yet to allow the tribespeople the opportunity of using discernment until they are certain whether the guest is friend or enemy. Thus, into this basic fabric of hospitality has been woven an ingenious thread of signs and signals—all part of the wilderness code of hospitality. Even though the desert abounds in brigands and thieves, human life is still sacred and cherished for all, if possible.

The code of hospitality recognizes that no man can exist alone in the wilderness. It is one of the deep truths learned in tough times. We are not only forced to lean on each other for help, but we are obligated to reach out to the stranger who knocks at our door.

It was this lesson Prince Moses learned from old Jethro. A well, which took a man many months to dig, is his. But the water belongs to all men. The unwritten law of the desert forbids a man putting a fence around a well or spring.

The same is true of shade. If a straggling pilgrim comes to your tree or tent, he is always welcome to sit and rest. To deny shade to a stranger, as the sun broils and the *sharav* or *hamsin* (hot wind off the desert) blows like the breath of a furnace, could mean quick death. Likewise, the warmth of an evening fire belongs to all who cross the wilderness. No man is left outside in the freezing winter elements but is always welcomed into the warm tent.

When a modern pilgrim crosses the Sinai wilderness and comes upon the tomb of a sheikh, its whitewashed dome visible for many miles, he will also find nearby a *maqad*, or hospice house. This one-room stone building with a sand floor is for hospitality. No one knows as the wilderness dweller does how important it is to have a place of refuge from the elements. Inside will be a fireblackened teakettle or *finjan*, several small pots and pans for cooking, some dried camel dung for a fire, perhaps some tea or ground coffee, herbs, a jug of water, some rice and maybe a store of flour to make pita. Those who eat and are refreshed are expected to return as soon as possible to replenish the pantry. If not, when the tribe gathers once a year at the tomb of the sheikh, they will replenish the supplies in the *maqad*.

As usual, all things are free.

Desert courtesy captures this truth: there are some things that belong to God, and thus belong to all people. It is the lesson of hospitality—the lesson of sharing.

It would have been natural for Moses to have withdrawn into a shell of self-pity when he left Egypt. But, as the psalmist reminds us, God sets the solitary in families (Psalm 68:6). Such families are not like prisons, with wardens constantly checking and requiring. Families are freeing institutions, opening the doors and windows of the jails into which we withdraw when we are alone.

To Moses God gave the family of Jethro. Intellectual reasoning, even preaching, were not enough to set Moses free from the bondage of grief and isolation. God knew Moses did not need preachments. He needed love. What he needed was what we all need—an arm around his shoulder, a soft bosom on which to lay his head, a good meal, fellowship in a family and a gentle voice saying, "I understand." Beyond that man cannot go, but God stands at the door beckoning.

In our wilderness wanderings we will eventually learn that. We will learn to diminish our preaching, refrain from advice and directions, and follow the example of Jethro: "Why did you leave him alone? Invite him to have something to eat."

Of such is the Kingdom of heaven. It is a free gift from the *maqad*, a gift we shall one day replenish when we pass this way again.

II

God's Call

*. . . and he led the flock to the backside of the desert, and
came to the mountain of God. . . .   (Exodus 3:1, KJV)*

There is a day in every life that comes unannounced, un-
heralded. No trumpets sound, there are no lightning flashes—but as we look back on it, we realize that day was the
turning point of our life.

That special day for Moses began as all other days in the
wilderness. For weeks the 80-year-old man had been moving
his scraggly flock of sheep and goats through the deep wadis
of the southern Sinai.

The rising sun climbed the back of the far-off peaks in
Midian, mountains red and purple with shades of lavender
and gray. Over there, beyond the deep waters of the Gulf of
Aqaba, was the land of Esau. Esau, the man with the ginger-
colored hair, who never fully inherited the birthright stolen by
his brother, Jacob.

Moses awoke and stretched. Even at 80, he was in remarkable physical condition. The discipline of the desert and proper nutrition—both helped account for his excellent health. He
had already outlived his debauched counterparts in long-
forgotten Egypt.

Lying comfortably in the soft sand of the enclosed wadi, he
watched his mixed flock of sheep and goats scattering out
ahead of him, searching for grass. It was time, he thought, to
find new pasture.

The sun rose higher, illuminating the huge mountain ahead of him. For two weeks he had been making his way inland from the coastal village of DiZhav through Wadi Nasb. It was a favorite grazing spot, for the winter floods washed grass seed from the high mountainsides down into the basin of the canyon, where it sprouted as fodder for his flocks. Each day he had climbed higher and higher into the mountain passes. This morning, as the sun reflected off the massive range ahead of him, he knew it was time to press on to greener pastures. He was particularly eager to push through the pass and emerge onto the high inland plain of *er Rakha*, where his flocks could feed for days.

As the sun continued its rise, an auroral orange filled the wadi, then flashed like a brilliant shard of flaming metal against the sides of the red mountain before him. Almost instantly the entire southern massif of the ancient, empty peninsula was bathed in the white heat of the next day.

Moses arose and, whistling for his flock, watched with satisfaction as they ran toward him, falling into line behind him as he moved forward toward the base of the towering granite mountain. All passage through the Sinai is done through the wadis—rough, circuitous saw cuts through the desert mountains. The wadis double as dried riverbeds and remain parched except for one or two days of those rare years when, in keeping with the antipodal extremes in the Sinai, they course with murderous, bubbling flashfloods that roll boulders, palm trees, entire Bedouin encampments toward the sea many miles beyond and below.

Shouldering his pack and checking to make certain his goatskin still contained water, Moses moved slowly westward, the sun at his back. As the wadi narrowed, its massive rock walls displayed the sharp, delicate and splintered violence that is common throughout the wilderness. The hills lie at broken angles to everything around them, sedimentary lines all turned sideways and pointing down toward the specific fault that twisted them.

Suddenly the sun crested the mountains behind him and the wadi was filled with searing heat. The goats, more agile than the sheep, were climbing the steep sides of the canyon. They avoided the bitter caper plants—known as hyssop—that grew in the cracks and crevices, but munched on other scarce vegetation. Moses, realizing the foolishness of remaining in the blistering sun, allowed his flock to graze as he stopped in the shade of an outcropping rock to watch. It was a day like so many other days over the last forty years.

The sun climbed quickly to its zenith, its scorching light illuminating every crack, every aperture of the landscape. The sheep and goats browsed as they had every other day, nibbling at the scant herbage. Nothing seemed to indicate this day was to be different from any of the other days.

Moses turned and looked to his left at the giant form of the triple-peaked mountain that arose abruptly from the wadi. In front of him, spread out like a huge flat dish, was the plain of *Er Rakha*. It had taken Moses all these years to get accustomed to the awful silence. Only vaguely could he recall the chirping of the crickets and katydids, the rumble of the bullfrogs and bellowing of the crocodiles in Egypt. Egypt had disappeared forever into the past. He thought of his older brother, Aaron, and Miriam, his sister. Were they still alive back in Egypt? Surely his mother and father had long since passed away. It made no difference. Now he had a new family: Zipporah, his wife, and his two sons, Gershom and Eliezer, now grown almost to manhood. Like his old father-in-law, Jethro, Moses had become a Bedouin. His life centered around the mundane—caring for his wife and children, tending his sheep and goats.

Moses leaned back against the rock and closed his eyes, holding his five-foot staff loosely. Jethro had told him tales of this place, of a mountain that roared, of the voice of the God Jethro called "El" that was sometimes heard in the absolute silence at the base of the mountain.

Through his closed eyelids, Moses was suddenly aware of another light, different from the sunlight. Gradually he opened his eyes and looked toward the base of the great mountain. A bush had burst into flames. This was not an uncommon sight during the heat of summer, as the dried bushes sometimes caught the isolated rays of the sun magnified through the quartz crystals lying randomly on the ground and burst into flames. Quartz crystals were common in this area of the Sinai, and Moses had often used them to refract the sun's rays to start his own fire of dried camel dung.

But there was something different about this fire. The

thornbush, which was green, was burning brightly—but it was not consumed. The fire itself seemed to be ethereal, ghostly.

There was a time in Moses' life many, many years before when he would not have had time to check out such a sight. In fact, he would have been so busy with his tasks in the Egyptian court, he probably would not have even noticed it. But the years in the wilderness had changed all that. Now there was time to smell the tiny wildflowers, to stop and talk to the small creatures of the desert, to fondle his sheep and goats, to carve figures from acacia wood or hew them from the easily shaped sandstone. It had taken years, but now Moses had slowed down enough from the maddening pace of life to have time to stop and listen.

"I will go over and see this strange sight—why the bush does not burn up," he mused.

From that moment, all his life was altered. The door, which had been closed so long it resembled the wall, suddenly opened. For as he approached the bush, a voice spoke, calling him by name: "Moses, Moses!"

That voice still speaks to wilderness wanderers. Though the day may seem to be a day like every other day, and the bush like all bushes, things are not always as they seem. Elizabeth Barrett Browning captured the concept:

> Earth's crammed with heaven,
> And every common bush afire with God;
> But only he who sees takes off his shoes. . . .

The tragedy of our wilderness experience is not that we have to go through grief and suffering, but that we often miss the blessings from burning bushes—the things through which God speaks. Through a letter from a friend, the words of a book, a long-forgotten song, the voice of a teacher, the beauty of a holy life, the innocence of a child, God still calls us by name and makes His eternal purpose known.

Even then, though we may see the miraculous and hear in the midst of it a voice calling our name, nothing is fulfilled until we respond. The Scriptures are full of stories of divine summonses, and of the men who responded—men like

Moses who had been prepared and were now ready to be used.

Learning to wait patiently, learning to do today what your hand finds to do, learning to hear the call of God when it comes, and to respond—that is what the wilderness is all about. Once a man submits his life to God's control, he voluntarily surrenders the right to determine or the power to vary the consequences of that decision. From that moment on, no situation can ever come into the life of the believer which has not first passed through the hands of God and thus has redeeming quality.

Our task, even though we may be wandering in some wilderness, is to remain ready. Our lamps should never be allowed to run low on oil, for who knows when a summons may come? Blessed is the free, unengaged spirit who has not encumbered himself with the things and cares of this world, who can at once put aside all he is doing to answer the call of God.

Many years later the prophet Isaiah would encourage a battered people to "wait upon the Lord." Waiting, Isaiah said, would bring renewed strength. While *wait* in the Hebrew has several connotations, the word used in Isaiah 40 means to be entwined about, to become part of. It is best illustrated by looking at a braided rope that is actually several strands woven together to become one large, strong strand. Though the smaller ropes are actually separate, they become one because they have been entwined and twisted together.

Moses had spent forty years waiting. But the waiting was not limited to the passing of time. It had to do with faithful service to Jethro—and the task before him. He had learned that service to God often means nothing more than doing with all his might what his hand found to do.

Waiting on the Lord, as one does in a wilderness experience, means we should become entwined with Him, braided into Him, as we become part of Him and He becomes part of us.

The burning bush gave direction to Moses' life—a life that for eighty years had been spent in preparation. He had been called by God, handed a commission, and sent forth to accomplish a task.

To all those wandering in the wilderness, let it be said: bushes still catch on fire and God still calls men by their names. But the call comes only to those who are busy with the smaller tasks already assigned.

III

Spiritual Authority

The Lord said to him, "What is that in your hand?" "A staff," he replied.

(Exodus 4:2)

When God needs a tool for His service, He usually looks for something common to use. He doesn't reach for a knife that is "factory-sharpened"; He prefers to hone His own edge out of rough metal.

The apostle Paul was the most unlikely man imaginable to carry the gospel to the Gentile world. He was not only a Jewish Pharisee; he was an ardent persecutor of Christians. But a touch from God changed all that on the road to Damascus.

Who would have thought the Messiah would have been heralded by a wild prophet who roamed the wilderness dressed in skins, eating locusts and wild honey? Or that the Messiah would have submitted to such a man for water baptism? Yet Jesus said of John the Baptist, "Among those born of women there is no one greater than John."

When Samuel went to the house of Jesse in search of God's choice for a king over Israel, he wound up anointing with oil the runt of the litter. All the other boys had kingly appearances, but the youngest son was ruddy, with red hair and freckles—a simple shepherd boy with slingshot and harp. Yet because of the touch of God, David was called "a man after God's own heart."

When God needed a man to defeat the Midianites, He turned to a confessed coward hiding behind the winepress. But the touch of God turned Gideon into a "mighty warrior." Rahab, a prostitute in Jericho, became the mother of all Israel. Out of her came the house of David, which eventually produced the Messiah.

Thus it is not unusual that God would choose a murderer who had just finished serving a forty-year prison term in the wilderness to lead His people from slavery into the Promised Land. Nor is it unusual that instead of putting a golden scepter into his hand, He transformed Moses' wooden shepherd's staff into the "rod of God."

The call of God at the burning bush was so radical, so unexpected, that Moses had difficulty comprehending. He did not doubt God, but he genuinely feared that when he tried to tell others, they would not believe.

It was then God asked that classic question: "What is that in your hand?"

"Only a walking staff," Moses replied.

Even the casual reader of the Bible can almost hear God chuckle. Chances are it was the same heavy wooden stick Moses had used to murder the Egyptian slavemaster. Later he had used it to thump the heads of the bully-shepherds harassing Jethro's daughters. But across the years, the five-foot staff had become not a weapon but a companion. It was hard to imagine Moses without his staff. Now God indicated it was to become something far more than a simple staff.

"Throw it on the ground," God told Moses.

Instantly it was transformed into a viper. Moses jumped back. But God, whose voice demanded absolute obedience, told Moses to pick it up by the tail. Instantly the snake was transformed back into a staff.

In Egypt the serpent occupied a central role in temple worship. When Moses, at God's command, picked up the serpent, it was a sign—not to others who might not believe, but to Moses himself. At the word of God, the serpent of Egypt would become a staff in the hand of Moses. All Moses had to do was to obey God at every turn. If he would do that, even when he was commanded to do the ridiculous or the dangerous, Pharaoh and the whole force of the Egyptian empire would be his to wield as easily as he wielded his staff.

Thus the shepherd's staff was transformed into a rod of spiritual authority, from that time on to be called the "rod of God." That "rod of God," in the hands of a man of God, would open seas, bring water from mountains and defeat the army of Amalek. Yet there was another lesson Moses forgot: in every rod there is a serpent. If authority is misused, the serpent strikes, and the bite is often deadly for the man holding the rod. Only once did Moses abuse his authority. As an old man he used his rod in anger—to strike a rock to bring forth water, rather than speak to it. God did not remove him from leadership, nor did He punish him, but Moses forfeited the right to enter the Promised Land. Such is the penalty of abusing God's power, for unto whom much is given, much is required.

The principle of the transformed staff, however, remains absolute. God is ever transforming the secular into the sacred, storing His heavenly treasure in earthen vessels, touching the common things and causing them to shine with His glory. A ram's horn, an ox goad, an earthen pitcher, a shepherd's sling, a lowly manger, five loaves and two fishes, an old rugged cross—God delights in using the foolish to confound the wise. A rod with God behind it is mightier than all the armies that ever marched—as Pharaoh was painfully to discover.

Forty years earlier Moses had not been ready. Then he thought he could correct all the injustice of Egypt—and the injustice of the desert—by using his rod as a weapon. Now that murderer's tool had been transformed, as had the murderer himself. It took the wilderness to purify, prepare and process the man of God. During that time, the stick in his hands lost its potency as a weapon and became a simple staff. He used it to climb the mountains, to beat the low brush in which the lambs were caught, to kill snakes, to chase off wolves and hyenas, to hold out over his sheep and count them as they came to the well to drink. Yet through all those forty years, God was forging a leader who did not need a sword to enforce authority.

Spiritual leaders are never elected; they are called by God. When God calls, He also equips, and makes the ministry fruitful. How can you tell if a man is a shepherd? Look behind him to see if there are sheep who know his voice and are following. The true shepherd has a flock. The rest are simply hirelings. His badge of authority may be a simple staff, but if he is called, that staff holds in it the awesome authority of God—an authority recognized by all.

In Moses' case, as with his ancestor Jacob, the symbol of authority was once a symbol of sin and selfishness. After his midnight encounter with an angel, Jacob forever walked with a limp, so others would know he had been touched by God. So Moses carried a blood-stained staff, now the symbol of moral purity and uprightness.

That, by the way, was the meaning of the second sign God gave Moses at the burning bush. God told Moses to put his hand into his robe. When he pulled it out, it was leprous—the symbol of sin. But when he put his hand back into the folds of his robe and withdrew it, it was cleansed. So God told Moses that never again would he have to hang his head in shame over past sin. As easily as God could change a serpent into a staff, so He could heal disease and forgive sin.

The fact that Moses' symbol of authority was a staff and not a scepter is significant. God did not appoint Moses king. He was to be an apostle, a spiritual father, a chief shepherd. That meant he would not use the kind of kingly authority that comes from perfect things—like scepters made of gold—but authority filtered from God through the commonplace.

The staff itself—bent, gnarled, chipped from many years of service—was a constant reminder to Moses of God's grace. No leader is perfect; so God takes the imperfect and through it accomplishes His perfect will. As one old Bible teacher used to say, "God can strike a lot of straight blows with a crooked stick."

The staff was an encumbrance as well. All the other leaders in Egypt carried swords or spears. But Moses was instructed to approach Pharaoh carrying his staff. He was to be deliberately conspicuous, out-of-place, so God's glory could be evident.

That is one of the prices of leadership. Moses could no longer act like a follower. He had been designated as a leader. As such, his behavior would always be different. The leader

cannot enjoy the luxury of living like a follower. He cannot
pretend he is not a leader. Leadership encumbers.

Moses realized this and did all he could to escape the call of
God and the responsibilities of leadership. He argued with
God: "Who am I, that I should go to Pharaoh?" Then he said
he didn't know God's name, that the people wouldn't believe
him without some kind of sign, and that he was not an elo-
quent speaker. Finally he wailed, "O Lord, please send someone else to do it" (Exodus 4:13).

God cut him short. "The Lord's anger burned against
Moses." Moses had said too much. God had called and there
was no escaping the call.

David knew how impossible it was to run away from God's
call:

> Where can I go from your Spirit?
>   Where can I flee from your presence?
> If I go up to the heavens, you are there;
>   if I make my bed in the depths, you are
>   there.
> If I rise on the wings of the dawn,
>   if I settle on the far side of the sea,
> even there your hand will guide me,
>   your right hand will hold me fast.
>   (Psalm 139:7-10)

When Moses left the burning bush, he was no longer carrying a staff. He had in his hand the rod of God. Nor was he any
longer a wanderer: he was a leader. It was time to return to
Jethro, inform him that the God of no name and no image
had appeared at the base of Mt. Sinai and commissioned him
to a task. He was now a man under authority. He was a man
of authority.

Often we shrink from the call of God, fearing it will deprive
us of pleasure, cause us to be ridiculed, force us from the
comforts of home into a rigorous life of discipline. As such, we
often equate the call of God with going to our doom.

Yet for each of us, God has something far greater than living
out our lives in the wilderness. In Moses' case, it was a life
filled with the excitement of the extraordinary. There would

be a great song of victory on the banks of the sea, an appointment with God on a mountaintop, being recognized as a worker of miracles and a healer of those bitten by serpents. He would receive a vision of glory, would be buried by the hand of an archangel, and would receive the supreme honor of standing with the Lord Jesus on the Mount of Transfiguration. Moses was called not to doom but to glory.

God honors simple things. He honors the man, the woman, who does what needs to be done, regardless of what it costs. He honors the person who, putting his hand to the plow, does not turn back. He honors the person who does today what his hand finds to do, and does it with all diligence.

The person constantly wishing for a better station in life seldom achieves. Somehow his big dream of the future often blocks a man from accomplishing the little things demanded by the present. But God never skips steps. He does not hopscotch through life, jumping over squares to miss the rock. He hits every step and brings us up through the ranks one grade at a time until we are ready to assume the task for which He has been preparing us all along.

"What is that in your hand?"

Something common, no doubt. Perhaps something stained with the sin of the past. But when God touches it, it becomes the symbol of authority.

> . . . There is hope for a tree:
>   If it is cut down, it will sprout again,
>   and its new shoots will not fail.
> Its roots may grow old in the ground
>   and its stump die in the soil,
> yet at the scent of water it will bud
>   and put forth shoots like a plant.
>
> (Job 14:7-9)

IV

Hidden Promises

When they came to Marah, they could not drink its water because it was bitter.   (Exodus 15:23)

God never brings a hindrance into our lives that He does not intend to be used to open another door that would not have opened otherwise.

When God spoke to Moses at the burning bush at the base of Mt. Sinai, commissioning him to return to Egypt to lead the Israelites out of bondage, He had a clear-cut plan. He said He was concerned about the suffering of the Israelites. He said He had come to rescue them and take them to a land of milk and honey. He said He would not forsake them as they traveled and would bring them to Mt. Sinai to worship Him (Exodus 3:7-12).

But such promises are hard to remember when you run out of water in the desert.

Even Moses doubted in the beginning. Returning to Egypt, he encountered great opposition, not only from the Egyptians but from the Israelites he was trying to lead to freedom. In Exodus 5:22 he cries out to God: "O Lord, why have you brought trouble upon this people? Is this why you sent me? Ever since I went to Pharaoh to speak in your name, he has brought trouble upon this people, and you have not rescued your people at all."

Later, however, encouraged by the miracles God had

worked through him—miracles that finally forced Pharaoh to release the Israelite slaves—Moses was reassured.

The next crisis of his leadership came at the edge of the Reed Sea. (The "Red Sea" of Exodus 13:18 is an incorrect translation of the Hebrew *Yam-Suph*, which means, literally, "Sea of Reeds.") This is probably located in the vicinity of the Bitter Lakes just north of the Gulf of Suez, an area about five miles wide and between ten and fifteen feet deep. Here, even though the Egyptian army was in hot pursuit and the impassable waters were before them, Moses was able to assure the people: "Do not be afraid. Stand firm and you will see the deliverance the Lord will bring you today. The Egyptians you see today you will never see again. The Lord will fight for you; you need only to be still" (Exodus 14:13-14). In short: "Don't just do something, stand there!"

Yet the deliverance of the children of Israel through the parting of the sea, and the subsequent destruction of the entire Egyptian army, was still not enough to convince the people that God's word to Moses at the burning bush was real. No sooner had they finished their celebration on the shores of the sea than they found themselves once again on the move. Instead of leading the people across the northern Sinai by the *Via Maris* —the "way of the sea" (a much shorter and easier way to cross the wilderness in order to get to Canaan)—Moses turned south along the eastern shore of the Gulf of Suez. It was a journey he had made many times. He was returning to Mt. Sinai so the promise of God could be fulfilled that the people would worship Him at the Mountain of God.

According to Exodus 12:37, there were 600,000 adult males and their families, plus the priestly tribe of Levi and the various camp followers—including some Egyptians who wanted to flee the nation. If this is a correct translation, it would mean the Exodus number could reach close to three million. However, the geographical logistics simply do not allow room to move that many people through the narrow wadis of the peninsula.

Other scholars point out that the Hebrew word *eleph*, which is usually translated *thousand*, can also be translated *family*. That would give a much more realistic figure. In other places in the Bible, the word *eleph* means "military units," meaning the exact number of people is unknown, but they were accompanied by at least 600 armed men, or armed squadrons.

When we get to the book of Numbers, however, we find there were 22,273 male babies born during the first year of the wanderings. Thus the actual number in the Exodus remains a mystery. Certainly it was far less than the traditional figure of millions, but probably more than 15,000, as some suspect.

Regardless of size, the fact of Moses' leadership remains indisputable, and for the most part the route is still rather clearly marked.

I have traveled that route, south along the shore to the Gulf of Suez through the scorching sands of the wilderness of Shur and Etham. My first trip to this region was in late spring, about the same time of year the Israelites passed that way. The sun was quickly dehydrating my body and parching my throat as I came against the problem that faces all desert travelers— lack of water.

Three days is the maximum time the human body can go without water in the desert. I thought of those Israelites so many years before. At least I had a canteen—and there was additional water on the desert vehicle that had gone on before. Those Israelites, however, had quickly run out of water after they left Egypt. Stretched to their absolute limit, the people were about to die when ahead they spotted the palm trees that marked the location of an oasis. Gasping, falling over each other, the cattle and flocks stampeding, they ran the last few feet toward the waters of Marah. There they fell on their faces beside the tepid pool.

Suddenly a great cry went up from the parched throats of the people kneeling beside the water. It was bitter. "Now," they cried, "we shall surely die of thirst!"

Moses was a seasoned guide. For forty years he had lived in that wilderness. He knew every watering place, every path through the wilderness. Surely he knew about the springs along the Gulf of Suez.

These springs are the same today as they were in Moses' time. When I reached Marah that hot afternoon, I found the same thing the Israelites discovered. The water of the springs, although clear and beautiful to look at, was laced with calcium and magnesium. This high mineral content makes the water so bitter it is almost impossible to drink.

Bending beside the spring, I ran my fingers through the water. It actually felt oily to the touch. All around the edge I could see the powdery white mineral residue where the rock sides of the spring touched the water.

"The Bedouins have a saying," my guide laughed. "'One spoonful and you go for a week.' In fact," he continued, "be careful not to lick your fingers now that you've put them into the water. The mineral is so potent your stomach will cramp in just a few minutes."

I quickly wiped my fingers on my shirt. Having experienced once before the awesome power of that bitter water in my intestines, I was not eager to replay the scene.

The actual location of Marah remains a mystery. Far to the south, near el Tur, is a place called "The Springs of Moses." This, according to the Arabs, is "Marah." There, in an old bathhouse, hot springs bubble from the ground into a covered pool. I have bathed in that water many times. It feels oily on the skin, and when it dries in the hot arid wind, it leaves a white powder all over your body. Despite the fact that there is bitter water at el Tur, however, it is far to the south of where the Israelites would have stopped after their first three days of travel from Egypt.

Most of the water along the Gulf of Suez is bad. On the other side of the peninsula, along the much deeper Gulf of Aqaba, the springs are usually sweet. But along the western side of the wilderness, near the relatively shallow Gulf of Suez, the water is filled with magnesium and other minerals. It is this combination of chemicals that constitutes the powerful laxative and causes intense and almost instant bowel problems.

The biblical account is stark and vivid. "For three days they traveled in the desert without finding water. When they came to Marah, they could not drink its water because it was bitter. [That is why the place is called Marah, which means 'bitter.'] So the people grumbled against Moses, saying, 'What are we to drink?'" (Exodus 15:22-24).

It was a desperate situation. All seemed destined to die.

Moses "cried unto the Lord." As an Egyptian he would have rebuked the people, demanding they drink. Or he might have threatened them. But his own wilderness time had changed his character. Full of patience, he turned instead to the One who had brought them to this place, to the One who hears every moan of agony from those He created. Surely God knew the water was bitter. Why then had He brought them this way?

God directed Moses to a nearby tree. Breaking the limbs to release the sap, he threw the wood into the water. The chemical reaction caused the minerals to precipitate to the bottom, leaving the water sweet to drink.

Beside each bitter Marah in the wilderness grows a tree that makes the water sweet. No wilderness pool is without such a tree. Poison and antidote, infection and cure, pain and relief, temptation and a way of escape—God always provides the sweet to remove the taste of the bitter. We do not always see it, but it is always there, if we are not too busy grumbling and complaining about the circumstances.

Yet somehow turning the water from bitter to sweet seemed to be God's second-best. Jesus, in the Garden of Gethsemane, had confessed He did not want to drink the "bitter cup," yet He surrendered to God's will. "Nevertheless," He prayed as He knelt in the dark night of His soul, "not my will but thine be done." By grumbling, the children of Israel had refused the bitter cup—and missed God's best purpose for their lives.

In Exodus 15:25, the historical account says the Lord was *testing* the people at Marah. In the Western concept, testing is for the purpose of ascertaining knowledge. It is used to determine how much one has learned. But the biblical concept of testing is not to ascertain knowledge; it is a method of teaching. When God "tests" His people, He is not doing so to find out whether they have learned their lesson and deserve a good grade. God's tests are learning experiences, designed by the Teacher to share knowledge, not to determine its presence or absence.

Thus, when God tested the people at Marah, He did it with a decree, not a questionnaire. He said, "If you listen carefully to the voice of the Lord your God and do what is right in his eyes, if you pay attention to his commands and keep all his decrees, I will not bring on you any of the diseases I brought on the Egyptians, for I am the Lord who heals you" (Exodus 15:26).

For almost half a millenium, God had been silent. Now He

had begun His progressive revelation of His nature and character to the people of earth. For the Jews, this would culminate with the giving of the law on Mt. Sinai. In the final analysis, God would fully reveal Himself through His Son, Jesus Christ. But it is significant to note that the first time God spoke to the people (He had spoken earlier to and through Moses), even before He thundered His law from Mt. Sinai, He revealed Himself as the Lord who heals sick bodies. Our God is a God who heals.

It is a marvelous promise that, like all God's promises, is conditional—found in the subjunctive mood and preceded by an *if*. The promise of the absence of disease is for those who (1) listen carefully to the voice of the Lord; (2) do what is right in His eyes; (3) pay attention to His commands; and (4) keep all His decrees. Only then does a man have the right to claim the promise of "none of these diseases."

An old Bible teacher used to remind his pupils that not only was the Lord interested in getting the people out of Egypt, He also wanted to get Egypt out of the people. That, perhaps, is at the heart of all wilderness experiences. In this case, the people had brought a lot of Egypt with them—internally. Egypt was a filthy nation. The entire nation had just undergone a siege of flies, locusts, dead frogs, boils and impure water. In the resulting plague, hundreds of thousands of Egyptian children had died. The Israelites, for the most part, had escaped the plagues. But they had still brought with them the contamination of Egypt. These included not only amoebic dysentery, but bilharzia, a weakening disease borne by snails in the slow-moving irrigation ditches of the Nile Valley (which still affects eighty percent of the peasants of Egypt). Now at Marah, the Lord spoke and told them He would not allow the Egyptian diseases to afflict them—if they but obeyed Him.

What did God want the Israelites to do? Obviously He wanted them to drink the water of Marah. But it was filled with magnesium. True, but even Moses could not have known about the medicinal qualities of calcium and magnesium. For one thing, magnesium is a powerful laxative. It was God's way of cleaning out their systems. Had they drunk the bitter water, and continued to drink it despite its effects on their intestines, their bodies would have ceased the purgative action and grown accustomed to the water. In the process, however, they would have expelled most of the amoeba, parasites and death-dealing germs they brought with them from Egypt.

There is another medicinal quality about the water of Marah. Calcium and magnesium form the basis of a drug called *dolomite*. Dolomite pills are used by professional athletes who perform in the sun. It is basically a muscle control drug to be used in extremely hot weather. Joggers, tennis players, those who exert themselves in hot weather often take dolomite to control muscle spasms. It is also used by patients with heart problems to control the heart muscle and keep it from going into fibrillation, which is the muscle beating out of control.

God had provided just the right medicine, not only to clean out the systems of the former slaves, but to prepare their bodies for the long and arduous journey through the desert. Thus their first stop in the wilderness journey was not a place of despair but a place where God had provided medicinal water.

We find later in the Exodus account that despite God's proclamation that "I am the God who heals thee," many of the people died of disease during the wilderness wanderings. Does that mean the promise of God was not valid? No, it simply points out the conditional nature of all God's promises. Often what seems foolish in our eyes is part of God's higher plan. Drinking the water of Marah did not make sense. But God had a plan far greater than man's desire to escape intestinal discomfort and a puckered mouth.

Over and over we are reminded that the reason for wilderness experiences is purification and preparation. The waters of Marah would have certainly brought almost instant purification. God was about to change the entire eating structure of the nation. No longer would they gorge themselves on shellfish, pork and the highly spiced foods of Egypt. To accomplish this change, God started with a purge, ridding them of all their perverse yearnings and desires. He was about to introduce them to their new dietary structure known ever since as "kosher." But the people rebelled at the first test. Thus the promise of a people without disease had to wait for a generation who listened carefully to the voice of the Lord and did not grumble at His commands.

The principle holds true even today. God wants us not only to live, but to live abundantly. His desire is for us to have long, productive and creative lives. So He continually leads us back to the waters of Marah where our crusty spirits may be broken—that the Spirit of God may enter.

V

Living Waters

Then they came to Elim, where there were twelve springs and seventy palm trees, and they camped there near the water.
(Exodus 15:27)

Shortly after the Six-Day War in 1967, Dr. Yitzhak Gutterman, a well-known desert botanist, and a group of Israeli researchers conducted a survey of the southern Sinai. While passing through Ras G'ara, near the Gulf of Suez, they spotted some corpses blackened by the desert sun. They were the remains of Egyptian soldiers who had retreated on foot from Sharm el Sheikh at the southern tip of the Sinai and were trying to reach their own lines. The unscarred bodies left no doubt to Dr. Gutterman that the soldiers had not died of battle wounds but from lack of water. Tragically, there was water less than twenty yards from where the soldiers had fallen along the sandy coast. But it was underground—and only a man familiar with the wilderness would have known how to find it.

Following that incident, Dr. Gutterman dedicated his life to helping others find water in the desert.

Every wilderness wanderer knows that water is the source of life. Without it, life in the desert is always on the brink of death.

Desert plants are uniquely adapted to live with scarce water. Their spiny leaves and tough surfaces mean less evaporation. The acacia tree, that sturdy thorn tree that seems to grow in the most desolate places, is capable of putting down roots more than thirty feet to find water. Even the smaller plants, such as the scuffy brown rotem bush, send out a huge root system and draw water from deep in the earth. Often I have dug around the base of a bush with green leaves and discovered water near the surface. I have also discovered the secret of covering the branches of a rotem bush with a plastic bag. In the cool of the evening this will produce enough water in a few hours through condensation to keep a man alive.

Desert animals are also adapted to live without water. The camel, which made its appearance in the Sinai about the time of the Exodus, is especially adapted. Although the longest documented trek of a camel between watering points is nearly 600 miles in 21 days, the Bedouin know it can go even longer if necessary. Contrary to popular opinion, the camel does not store water in its hump. Water is stored in the red corpuscles of the bloodstream, which can expand to 240 times their original volume when the camel drinks. After long periods without water, the camel is capable of drinking over 400 pints of water at one time, which is immediately distributed through the entire body, restoring his water loss in just a few minutes.

Human beings do not fare as well in the desert. The Bedouin have learned the necessity of covering the entire body to prevent an abnormal loss of water. Black robes, incidentally, actually lower the skin temperature and prevent even more evaporation. Often I have had to compel my companions to drink from their canteens, even though they did not feel thirsty; for on a hot day a person climbing in the desert can lose more than four quarts of water in one hour. Even while resting in the desert shade, the human body excretes more than two quarts of water in an hour. Man in the desert is always on the brink of death.

The children of Israel had never been thirsty before they began their desert trek. Despite the fact that the water of Egypt was polluted, there was always enough of it. The mighty Nile never went dry.

The desert, though, was different. Here the sun drew moisture from their bodies at an incredible rate. Leaving Egypt in the middle of the month of *Nissan*, which corresponds to the first week of April, they encountered desert temperatures of

100 degrees F. By the middle of *Tammuz*, three months later, midday temperatures would soar past 120. Only the strong could survive.

Death by dehydration does not come rapidly. It creeps up on you. Even the seemingly natural sign of thirst is absent. I remember one evening when one of the men in a group I was escorting through the desert almost died of dehydration. Early that morning, before we left the safety of our vehicle for a steep mountain climb, I warned those in the small party of the dangers of dehydration. I told them to drink water from their canteens every half-hour, whether they were thirsty or not.

That night we camped in a box canyon. I noticed that one of the men, normally active and full of vitality, seemed sluggish and lethargic. His voice was slurred and he finally left the circle of men around the campfire, saying he was not hungry. In a few moments I heard him in the darkness, heaving with violent nausea.

While one of the men rolled out his sleeping bag on the sand, I questioned him about the day's activities. Had he been drinking water? No, he said, he didn't like water. He preferred coffee. Had he urinated during the day? Yes, but only once. What was the color of his urine? A dark brown, he confessed, almost like syrup. He was close to death.

We quickly tucked him into his sleeping bag to prevent any more moisture loss to the dry desert air. Then we began the slow process of replenishing the liquids in his body—liquids he insisted he did not want to drink. We started with salty soups. Then water. Within two hours he was feeling better. Before he went to sleep, the doctor in our group fixed a two-gallon container of medicated water, which he put beside the head of his sleeping bag.

"When I wake in the morning," he told my foolish friend, "I want that container empty. I will wake you every hour during the night and expect you to drink a quart at a time. If you don't, you may not wake at all when the sun rises."

It was ample motive to drink.

Similar problems face us as we move through our spiritual wilderness. Spiritual thirst, the need for living water, is the dominating factor in the lives of all human beings. It begins with a deep longing for something to satisfy inner cravings.

Although we realize that Jesus said the man who "hungers and thirsts after righteousness shall be filled," we are often shocked to find we are thirsting for the wrong things. We don't want righteousness; we prefer selfish gain and pleasure. The desire pursues us from Egypt and tracks us across the deserts of our lives, until we cry out as Paul did: "When I want to do good, evil is right there with me. . . . What a wretched man I am! Who will rescue me from this body of death?" (Romans 7:21-24).

In fact, it is these very cravings that cause many of us to behave in such a way that we are forced into the wilderness to begin with.

In his concept of the "God-shaped vacuum," St. Augustine once prayed, "Our hearts are restless until we find our rest in Thee." Thus, while it is thirst that drives us forward, we are never satisfied, no matter how much we drink, until we drink from the fountain of Living Water.

The children of Israel, with Marah behind them, staggered on through the desert sands along the Gulf of Suez. Their thirst had returned as the days grew longer and hotter. Slowly the great procession turned inland, following the directions of Moses who had been this way many times before. Ahead lay the huge red and brown mountains of the southern Sinai. With weary feet the Israelites climbed the gentle slopes of a sandy alluvial plain which fanned from a narrow wadi and emptied into the Gulf of Suez behind them. Climbing, slipping over pebbly ground, their lips parched, their bodies fatigued, they were close to death. Slowly the long procession funneled into the narrow wadi between two huge red mountain ranges and disappeared inland.

No one knows exactly where Elim is. Chances are it was in what is now Wadi Feiran, where still exists one of the most beautiful oases in the Middle East. It is described in Scriptures as a "place where there were twelve springs and seventy palm trees" (Exodus 15:27). It was here the Israelites camped and were refreshed.

There are three basic sources of water in the desert: cisterns, wells and springs. While Elim was an oasis with springs, the Bedouin also hew cisterns and dig wells. The cistern system is ingenious. Through a pattern of ditches and aqueducts, they channel water from the intermittent rains into the basins for storage. The huge cisterns at the mountain fortress of Masada near the Dead Sea held millions of gallons of water collected in this way, which could be dipped to the top by buckets. At best, though, this was but a temporary way to store water.

In most cases, water in the desert is obtained from wells.

It was said of Jacob that everywhere he went, he built an altar and dug a well. The problem, of course, was knowing where to dig.

To the Bedouin this is a simple matter. It is said that the desert sand is to the Bedouin what the morning newspaper is to the Englishman—only with fewer misprints. He knows not only how to track, but where to find water.

As I stood beside an old Bedouin man one afternoon, he showed me, by studying the landscape, where he should dig his well. The mountains in the southern Sinai are volcanic. At some time in the past, the long, deep veins between the igneous rocks were filled with volcanic magma—forced up from deep in the earth under great pressure. When the magma cooled, it produced dark, black seams that streak across the mountain ranges at right angles to the wadis.

"Look there," the old man said, pointing at the side of the mountain. I saw the dark seams—black with spots of green and copper. "We call them *dykes.*"

I climbed up on the side of the ravine and could see this particular dyke extending across the desert for miles. It looked like the angry crayon mark of a small child as it contrasted against the light-colored granite and sandstone. To the side I noticed others only inches wide. This particular one was at least four feet wide. I knew it extended probably hundreds of feet into the earth.

Looking down on the old Bedouin, who was making a mark in the sand where his boys would come later to dig the well, I could see where the dyke intersected the floor of the wadi and disappeared into the ground. It then reappeared on the other side, snaking its way up the side of the cliff to continue its streak across the mountain range. That was evidence it had continued on under the sand bed of the wadi.

"When the wadi fills with water during the winter rain," the old man told me as we made our way back toward his tent, "much of the water soaks into the sandy bottom of the canyon. What is on the upstream side of the dyke forms an underground lake."

It was into this natural reservoir, trapped by the dam beneath the sand, he would dig his well. The presence of a date palm nearby was additional confirmation that there was water beneath the surface of the sand.

The digging would be tedious. It would take at least two men. One would dig with a shovel, shoring up the sides with rocks as he went down through the sand. The other would pull the excess sand to the surface in a bucket on a rope. I was glad the old Bedouin had not asked me to help. Going down thirty to sixty feet into a well was something I was quite content to let someone else do!

For the children of Israel, having to dig a well and then leave it behind was a wrenching process. To them God gave a magnificent promise, however, that one day He would bring them to a land with "wells you did not dig" (Deuteronomy 6:11).

One of the signs of entrance into the Promised Land is adequate spiritual nourishment. There may be giants and walled cities, but those who have entered the Promised Land will always be able to quench their spiritual thirst because of a covenant relationship with Christ. In the wilderness, however, one often has to dig his own wells.

It is not enough, in the desert, to depend on surface water—blessings that fall intermittently. Man needs a much deeper source of life than that brought by showers of blessings. He must have a source upon which he can draw when there has been no rain for years.

David wrote about the spiritual man who was "like a tree planted by streams of water, which yields its fruit in season" (Psalm 1:3). Interestingly, the Spanish Bible does not translate "streams" with the usual Spanish word *rio*. It uses the less common word *arroyo*. The river David was talking about was not a flowing stream but a dry gulch—a wadi. The spiritual man does not need constantly flowing water in order to prosper. He prospers even when the skies are cloudless and the land parched. He prospers because his roots, on the upstream side of the dyke, go deep into the sand and draw from the underground supply.

Cisterns are not adequate when the sun grows hot and there is no rain for years. Jeremiah warned the people of Israel about the danger of this. "My people have committed two sins," the Lord said through Jeremiah. "They have forsaken me, the spring of living water, and have dug their own cisterns, broken cisterns that cannot hold water" (Jeremiah 2:13).

Neither cisterns nor wells give a sure supply of water. Only the presence of a spring, where water flows freely of its own accord, affords certainty. Elim was such a place—with twelve springs surrounded by numerous date palms. This water was not collected by man's efforts, nor did it have to be drawn to the surface by man's efforts. It flowed freely for anyone who would come and drink.

Jesus was talking about this when He sat at Jacob's well in Samaria. In the story in John 4, He was sitting on the edge of a well when a Samaritan woman approached to draw water. In His conversation with her Jesus said, "Everyone who drinks this water will be thirsty again, but whoever drinks the water I give him will never thirst. Indeed, the water I give him will become in him a spring of water welling up to eternal life" (John 4:13-14).

The King James Version says, "A well of water springing up." But that is a poor translation. Jesus never talks about wells; He talks of springs. A well is something man has to dig. A spring is a gift from God. Religious people—Pharisees and others who feel they have to earn salvation—dig wells. The spring, like God's grace, bubbles up from underground of its own accord. You don't have to do anything to earn it. You don't have to labor for it. Like salvation, it is a free gift to all who stoop to drink.

At another time Jesus spoke more of this: "If a man is thirsty, let him come to me and drink. Whoever believes in me, as the Scripture has said, *streams* of living water will flow from within him" (John 7:37, italics added).

The writer says Jesus was speaking of the Holy Spirit who is never a cistern, never a well, but always a spring. He becomes a river flowing out of the heart of all those who come to Jesus and drink of Living Water.

The wilderness prepares us to become more than a vessel to hold water. In the wilderness we actually become a source of water for others.

For every Marah, there is an Elim just beyond. We are never bidden by God in our wilderness trek to continue to drink the bitter water. After the crucifixion comes the glorious resurrection. At Elim we rest. We encamp near the water. Here He makes His sheep lie down in green pastures and leads us beside the still waters. Here our soul is restored

What a God is ours! He drowns our foes in the sea and disciplines His children in the next breath. He leads us to the bitter waters of Marah, then urges us to move on to the cool shade of Elim. He thunders from the mountaintop but feeds His flock and gently leads those that are with young. In every desert there is an Elim. Here we pause, are refreshed, and move on to a land of streams and rivers.

VI

Discoveries

They left the Desert of Sin and camped at Dophkah.
                                                    (Numbers 33:12)

Every wilderness abounds with serendipities—accidental but wonderful discoveries. They come at least-expected times and in least-expected places, to encourage us in our trek through the tough times of life.

Who of us, struggling through some seeming desert waste or toiling up some peakless mountain, has not rounded a turn and come face-to-face with a marvelous little surprise—and from it drawn strength for the journey? No wilderness is without them.

I think of the time, shivering from the cold blast of winter that swirled off the side of Mt. Sinai with icy needles, I crawled into a deserted hermit's cave for warmth. There before me, as though some angel had seen me coming and laid it on an outcropping rock at the back of the cave, was a tattered Bible. It was open to the very passage in Isaiah from which this book takes its title: "I will even make a way in the wilderness, and rivers in the desert" (Isaiah 43:19, KJV). Those words not only warmed me that chilly afternoon, but sparked an idea that eventually became this book.

God has placed at select turns in our lives these unexpected, fascinating treasures to enrich our lives and give us hope that others have passed this way before us—and not only achieved victory but left behind a message of hope.

The Sinai is no exception, for it is a land of constant surprises, endless serendipities.

More than a thousand years before Moses slogged his way through his own personal wilderness, paying the penalty for his sin but being prepared for the history-changing situation that lay ahead, the Sinai was being occupied by a people who gave a name to the territory.

From the Chaldean city of Ur, the legendary home of the patriarch Abraham, came another man, Naram-Sin, the king of Akkad. Conquering the lands north of the Persian Gulf, he moved westward and occupied (according to a deciphered Assyrian fragment) a land he called Maganna ("the country of copper") and Milukkha ("the country of blue stone"). Blue stone, of course, is found in the vicinity of copper mines. It is called turquoise.

Naram-Sin headed a cult that worshiped the moon god Sin (pronounced *sign,* with no connection to the English word *sin).* They conquered and settled in the western portion of the wilderness peninsula along the Gulf of Suez. Across the years, their descendants were known by a variety of names. All of them, at one time or another, worshiped the moon god Sin. Thus the region along the Gulf of Suez became known as "the wilderness of Sin" and the entire peninsula was called Sin-ai.

Several hundred years after Naram-Sin settled in the Sinai, the family of Israel moved to Egypt to take up residence following a famine in Canaan. It was not long before their brother/benefactor Joseph died, and according to Exodus, "a new king, who did not know about Joseph, came to power in Egypt" (Exodus 1:8). He made slaves of the Israelites and put them to work at hard labor.

During this time, the Egyptians began expanding their borders and colonized the Sinai. They wanted to use the barren wasteland for two purposes—first, as a wall (or *shur)* to keep out invaders from the east. Second, they wanted to work the copper and turquoise mines that had been discovered originally by Naram-Sin. The greatest lode was found in the mountains that rise to the east of the Gulf of Suez, about halfway down the peninsula, at a place called Serabit el Khadim.

It was the vanquished children of Israel, of course, who were used as slaves to dig the mines in the sides of the high mountains. (Serabit el Khadim means "heights of the slave.")

For several hundred years the Egyptians carried on their lucrative mining operations at Serabit. This was interrupted when a group of Semitic people called Hyksos invaded Egypt through the Sinai and ruled the Nile Valley from about 1700 to 1580 B.C. During this time the Sinai mines at Serabit fell into disuse. After the Hyksos were driven from Egypt, however, the expeditions to the Sinai resumed, this time under military escort. A large garrison of Egyptian soldiers was stationed at Serabit to oversee the Israelite slaves.

Ironically, the Egyptians also worshiped, among other deities, a moon god called Thoth. The slaves were forced to build a temple at Serabit el Khadim to honor Thoth, who was represented on the walls as a baboon or ibis-headed figure. The primary deity of the temple, however, was the well-known Egyptian goddess of turquoise, Hathor. Hathor, who was also goddess of love, mirth and joy, was represented by a woman's body with the head of a cow.

A huge complex grew up around the Temple of Hathor, which included a courtyard, sanctuaries, purification baths, a sacrificial altar and a barracks area for the Egyptian soldiers who policed the slaves. Remains of the temple still stand on the top of the mountain at Serabit el Khadim, with numerous inscriptions in hieroglyphics—an unwieldy alphabet of picture-writing with more than 700 basic characters. This was augmented by some Egyptians who had also mastered the 300 Sumerian cuneiform symbols.

There is some evidence that Moses may have headed up an expedition of Egyptian soldiers or miners during the first forty years of his life, and perhaps he even visited Serabit el Khadim, which is also called Dophkah in the Bible. Later, when he led the children of Israel out of Egypt, he encamped at Dophkah. Sometime prior to the Exodus, however, the supply of copper and turquoise had been expended and the mines had been closed. The slaves were returned to Egypt to work in the clay pits.

To those Hebrews who had once slaved in those impossible conditions, who had seen their loved ones die in the mines from lack of water and exposure to the elements, who had been forced to help build the temple to the heathen gods and goddesses, it must have given great satisfaction to pass by on their way to the Promised Land—free.

Before the mines were closed, however, an extraordinary intellectual event occurred at Serabit. The Israelite slaves, although they spoke their original tongue—a crude type of Hebrew—had no written language. In fact, at that time, except for the Egyptian hieroglyphics, there were no written languages anywhere in the world, for no alphabet had yet been devised. While tradition credits the Phoenicians with the birth of the alphabet, later archaeological discoveries have revealed an amazing fact. Sometime between 1500 B.C. when the Egyptians reopened the mines and 1300 B.C. when the mines played out, these brilliant slaves did something no one else in the world had ever done: they developed an alphabet.

Sometimes the most creative things come out of wilderness experiences. This wilderness of hardship and slavery became the birthplace of our modern alphabet, the birthplace of writing as we know it today.

Conceivably it was the Levites who developed the alphabet. These priests, into whose hands had been entrusted the keeping of the memory of the God with no image and no name, the God of Abraham, Isaac and Jacob, were forced into slave labor in the sweltering turquoise mines of the desert. Yet there, in the most dismal conditions, they devised an alphabet. It was this same alphabet that another of their tribe, Moses, would use to write the first five books of the Bible, which included all the covenants, laws and ordinances of God.

This first alphabet, known as Proto-Canaanitic symbols, was a major departure from the hieroglyphics of the Egyptians. Instead of being merely pictures representing words, these were symbols representing basic consonantal sounds, from which an infinite variety of new words could be formed. This evolved into the Proto-Sinaitic alphabet, which formed the basis of the Phoenician alphabet, from which our own alphabet was derived.

It was also at Serabit el Khadim that I discovered my own serendipity.

A small group of us had climbed the 5,000-foot mountain to

view the caves and have a brief devotional service at the ruins of the temple to Hathor. The idea of worshiping the living Lord at the place where men once worshiped false gods was exciting.

But it was also sad. Wandering through the temple remains, I saw the place where sacrifices—perhaps human sacrifices— were offered to appease the heathen gods and goddesses. Higher up were the quarters where the sacred prostitutes satisfied the sexual appetites of heathen worshipers. No doubt these included Hebrew women forced into prostitution, especially the young teenage virgins brought from Egypt to satisfy the garrisoned soldiers.

I walked slowly through the ruins, my spirit hearing the cries that went up from those forced to profane the most sacred things of their lives. Was there no hope in this place? I groaned. Here on this isolated mountaintop, God's chosen people were treated worse than beasts of burden: abused, humiliated, used and finally killed.

I thought of the word God had given to Isaac: "Do not go down to Egypt; live in the land where I tell you to live. Stay in this land for a while, and I will be with you and will bless you. For to you and your descendants I will give all these lands and will confirm the oath I swore to your father Abraham" (Genesis 26:2-3).

But Isaac's grandchildren had sinned. Consumed with jealousy, they had sold their baby brother to slavetraders who had taken him to Egypt. As a result, the entire clan was eventually forced into Egypt also. The next ten generations suffered from the sins of their fathers.

Where were You, God? I questioned in my heart. *Where were You during all those years of hardship and deprivation?* There had been no spoken word from God for 400 years—from the time God spoke to Joseph until He spoke to Moses just a few miles from where I was standing. *Was it because these people had forgotten You? Had they turned their backs on You during this blackest time in their history?*

I wandered around the side of the mountain and there, on the path in front of me, like the dark eye sockets of a skull, was the entrance to the mines. I shuddered. What agony must have been suffered in those caverns! Old men, young boys, chained together as they dug in the sweltering heat, as their naked bodies shivered when the fierce winter winds swept across the mountaintops, covering their beards with ice. I looked out across the awesome landscape. How ironic—the place named for the moon goddess even looked like a moonscape. Was there no word from God ever heard during that horrible time?

My Jewish guide was motioning me to come forward. I stumbled along the narrow path on the side of the mountain and entered the farthest mine opening, a small, cavelike socket that dropped down through the red and brown rock into a huge open cavern.

The guide, a brilliant Jewish woman, was pointing. "There, on the ceiling and walls. Do you see it?"

The amber and red walls curved up to form a rock ceiling over our heads, barely giving us enough room to stand. Distinct on the walls were the ancient inscriptions—chisel marks where the Hebrew slaves had carved words using their newly developed alphabet.

I stood for a long time, looking. The characters were obviously a prototype of modern-day Hebrew. I could even recognize a few of the letters from my days in Hebrew classes in seminary. Archaeologists had long before determined its originality and authenticity. It was the oldest known inscription of the alphabet as we now know it.

I was standing at the birthplace of the alphabet.

"What does it say?" I asked my guide, perhaps the world's foremost authority on the Sinai.

She carefully pointed out inscription by inscription. "There are two messages," she said. "The first one contains practical instructions for the other miners. 'You shall give Abubu eight portions of. . . .'" The last words were obliterated.

I was stunned. It was one of the major purposes of all writing—to pass along practical instructions as an extension of the mind and voice. As it was now, so it was in the beginning.

"What about the other inscription?" I asked.

"It is a very simple message," she said. "Obviously written by one of the old Levi slaves. It says, 'God is eternal.'"

I stood for long moments staring at my serendipity. Here,

hundreds of years after God spoke His covenant to the father of these people, just a few miles from the spot where, many years later, He would thunder His laws and commands from Mt. Sinai, in the midst of the most miserable bondage the world has ever known—God had a man. He had revealed Himself, not to a pharaoh but to a humble slave miner who had left chiseled in stone the first words ever written—the eternal nature of God.

The turquoise of the Sinai was of poor quality. The Egyptians soon discovered that it faded and became worthless. All those years of digging in the earth left nothing to show except a brief message on the wall of a cave.

In every wilderness God has a witness.

VII

Changed Appetites

"If only we had meat to eat! . . . But now we have lost our appetite; we never see anything but this manna!"
(Numbers 11:4, 6)

The experienced desert traveler knows better than to spread his sleeping bag under a tree or near the base of a cliff. Spiders, scorpions, even snakes have been known to drop from the heights onto a sleeping man's face. The wise wanderer always sleeps in the open.

One of the men in our group, whom I'll call Hal, disregarded the warning. When we arrived at our camping place after dark, he was too weary from the day's journey to think of anything but rest. He unrolled his sleeping bag and placed it under the drooping boughs of a large tamarisk tree.

The next morning I wakened at dawn. Lying sleepily in my bag a few yards away from the tree, I heard Hal give a startled gasp. I sat up, saw he had camped under the tree, and immediately wondered if he had been bitten by a scorpion or snake. Then I heard our guide, a muscular Israeli soldier, laughing.

I scrambled out of my bag and ran toward the tree. Hal was prone in his bag, only his head poking out, his eyes darting in all directions. His sleeping bag was covered with dozens of white spots, each about the size of a half-dollar. I looked around and saw the same flaky wafers all over the ground near his head.

"What is it?" Hal asked, staring at the guide, who was standing over him chuckling.

"That's what it is," the guide answered with a wide grin.

"I said, 'What is it?'" Hal's fear had turned to irritation, for he sensed he was being mocked.

"That is what it is," the guide laughed. "It is called 'What is it?'" Then he motioned at the substance on the ground around the sleeping bag. "In Hebrew the word is *man hu*, which means 'What is it?' The Bedouin call it *mann*. Who knows, perhaps it is the manna of the Bible."

By that time the rest of the group had gathered and were picking up the little wafers, sticky and sweet, and tasting them. Of course the bottom side was covered with sand, and what had fallen on the sleeping bag had soaked in and hardened, leaving a real mess.

But at least it wasn't a scorpion or a snake.

In the southern Sinai from May to July, a tiny insect punctures the bark of the tamarisk tree, drinks the sap and exudes a clear liquid that solidifies as a sugary globule when it hits the ground. When the sun comes up, it melts quickly and disappears. The fact that it is called *man hu* or *mann* reminded us, indeed, of the manna of the Bible, which was described as "thin flakes like frost on the ground [which] appeared on the desert floor" when the dew disappeared in the morning. It was "white like coriander seed and tasted like wafers made with honey" (Exodus 16:14, 31).

Moses called it "bread" and told the people to gather it and eat it. It was God's provision since their food had run out. It would last them until they reached the Promised Land, just a few miles to the north. It could be ground in the mills or beaten in the mortars and boiled in pots or baked as cakes (Numbers 11:8). It was to be eaten the day it was gathered or it would spoil. Only on the day before the Sabbath could they gather enough for two days. It kept the Israelites alive—and healthy—for forty years in the wilderness.

Although it is an intriguing concept, I do not believe the present-day *mann* is actually the manna of the Bible, although it seems to be similar. The present *mann* is confined to the southern Sinai and found only in small quantities during the late spring months. The manna of the Bible fell abundantly throughout the year and was found as far north as Kadesh-Barnea, where the Israelites camped for 38 years during their wilderness trek. It was without doubt a miracle from God specifically for His chosen people.

Despite the fact it was "God's provision," it was anything but tasty. The Israelite women used great ingenuity to change its appearance—but manna every day was a radical change of diet to people who had grown accustomed to the spices and meats of Egypt.

The first encounter with manna came when the Israelites ran out of food after leaving Elim on their way to Mt. Sinai. There had been some more complaining in the camp. God seemed to understand and said to Moses, "I will rain down bread from heaven for you" (Exodus 16:4). It was another remarkable and miraculous evidence of a God who cared and was able to provide.

At the same time quail appeared, a special bonus of meat from the Lord. During the late spring—and this would have taken place in early July—huge flocks of quail often migrate from Africa over the Sinai on their flights north for the summer. It is not unusual to find them by the hundreds along the beaches, where they lie exhausted after their long overwater flight. Until restrictive laws were passed, the Bedouin often stretched low, long nets along the sand dunes near the shore to snare the weary, low-flying birds. But this time the quail came inland and literally fell at the feet of the Israelites, providing them with the best meal they had had since leaving Egypt.

While the quail did not reappear as a steady diet, the manna did. Every morning. Despite the fact it was God's divine provision, the Israelites soon grew tired of the same diet, and once again, after leaving Mt. Sinai on their way to Kadesh-Barnea, the grumbling resumed. This time God reacted sternly.

Moses had earlier warned the people about complaining. "You are not grumbling against us, but against the Lord," he told them point-blank (Exodus 16:8).

While they turned a deaf and rebellious ear to Moses' warning, God's reaction was unmistakably impressive. At a place called Kibroth-hattaavah—which means "graves of craving"—

quail appeared by the thousands. The people, instead of giving God praise, rushed out and stuffed themselves. This brought God's wrath upon them so that even while they were gorging themselves, many died.

Today, scattered throughout the Sinai, are strange, round, above-ground grave sites called *nawamis*. Archaeologists say these free-standing stone enclosures are the oldest existing above-ground structures in the world. Although they have long since been emptied by robbers and archaeologists, when first discovered they were filled with human bones. Tradition says they were the bones of the grumblers who were discontented with God's manna and lusted for the fleshpots of Egypt.

The tragedy of human history is that man never seems to learn from his mistakes, or the mistakes of those who have gone before him. The man who insists upon learning everything from personal experience will seldom make any progress. At worst, he will perish in the wilderness. The wise pilgrim builds on the past.

The human heart is the same in all generations, and Satan has no new tactics available. When the apostle Paul was writing to the church in Corinth of the events that happened to the children of Israel in the Sinai, he warned them not to repeat history. "God was not pleased with most of them," he wrote. "Their bodies were scattered over the desert" (I Corinthians 10:5).

Paul listed the things the Israelites did that displeased God: idolatry, pagan revelry, sexual immorality, presuming on God's goodness, and grumbling. "These things happened to them as examples and were written down as warnings for us. . . . So, if you think you are standing firm, be careful that you don't fall!" (I Corinthians 10:11-12).

It's significant that Paul lists grumbling as equal to pagan revelry, idolatry and sexual immorality. There is a school of thought that says it's all right to curse at God. "Get it off your chest," we are told. But such an attitude assumes God never responds to man's actions. The wilderness wanderings teach us otherwise. God has a keen ear. It is especially tuned to those caught in desert experiences, for God does not allow His children to experience the wilderness without purpose. Even the changing of our diet from meat to manna is part of God's greater plan for our lives.

God has a purpose for everything He does. There was purpose in the manna. At the bitter springs of Marah, He wanted to purge their systems. Next He purposed to change their diet. As at Marah, however, the people rebelled. They failed to see that God had a master plan, that nothing was left to chance. Had the Israelites stopped to think, they would have understood that God was pledged by the most solemn obligations to provide for them. They grumbled because they did not believe. Even as Jesus was unable to work miracles in Nazareth "because of their unbelief," so the Israelites missed God's blessing when they doubted and grumbled. For the sin of unbelief is the greatest of all sins. There is, of course, a difference between healthy dissatisfaction and grumbling. Grumbling against circumstances says, in essence, that God does not love us or He would not treat us this way.

Granted, manna was not what they ordered off God's menu. They wanted the food of Egypt. Yet God's ways are not our ways. His provision often looks superficial to the carnal mind. "If we're God's 'chosen people,' why do we have such a meager diet? We should eat like kings—like the pharaoh." It was the sin of presumption, for they felt they knew better than God what they should eat. They were too shortsighted to understand a God who insisted on closing the door to Egypt's food forever, and who was more interested in teaching them the discipline of obedience than in satisfying their carnal cravings.

Temptation, which in its basic form is always a desire to return to Egypt, demands a tempter—one who stimulates our minds away from God. The "tempters" in this case were those Egyptians who had been invited to join the Exodus when the Israelites fled Egypt. But they were not part of the covenant group. The Bible calls them "the rabble" or the "mixed multitude."

"The rabble with them began to crave other food, and again the Israelites started wailing and said, 'If only we had meat to eat! We remember the fish we ate in Egypt at no cost—also the cucumbers, melons, leeks, onions and garlic. But now we have lost our appetite; we never see anything but this manna!'" (Numbers 11:4-6).

Many of the laws given from Mt. Sinai dealt with mixing with unbelievers. Especially was marriage with unbelievers condemned. Jesus later pointed out that no man can serve two masters, and Paul talked about those "enemies of the cross" whose "god is their stomach . . . their mind is on earthly things" (Philippians 3:18-19). The Lord commanded His people to come apart and be a "separate people"—not to mix with "the rabble." But not only did the Israelites mix with them in the wilderness; they *listened* to them. And many joined them in their grumbling. "The rabble" desired the safety of the fellowship but were constantly campaigning for the best of Egypt as well. They were convinced but not converted.

The problem with mixed multitudes is differing appetites. Appetites are determined largely by family background. The Egyptians yearned for leeks and garlic, meat and melons; while Moses, who had spent the last forty years in the wilderness, was profoundly grateful for the gift of manna. Now, as the desert heat burned mercilessly on these wanderers, they remembered the temporary relief of Egypt's cooling melons and cucumbers. Unfortunately, they forgot the lash of the taskmaster and the agony of slavery.

When Moses refused to listen to their grumbling and requests to turn back, they rebelled. It was, in essence, a counterrevolution—a common problem faced by all revolutionary leaders whose followers, after the first victories, often grow discouraged over the sparse diet and long trek before reaching "the Promised Land."

God prescribed a strict diet of manna along with restrictions for gathering and storing. It was more than many could take. It's not that they wanted to return to bondage; they just wanted a quick respite into the past—an overnight excursion, so to speak, back into sin.

But such excursions are always forbidden by God, for they bring with them a rekindling of old tastes for things not healthy. Manna was not tasty. But God was changing tastes. He was transforming a group of sloppy, undisciplined former slaves into an army. There is no place for gourmet menus in

the wilderness. Here men exist on bare essentials—getting
their minds off their bellies and onto God.

This was made clear to me on my first excursion into the
Sinai. I had brought with me my teenage son, Bruce. Although he adapted well to the rigors of desert living, he was
constantly wishing (out loud) for an ice-cold carbonated
drink. Our guide was amused at this "American desire" and
pointed out the danger of such a drink in the desert.

"It tickles the throat and fools you into thinking your thirst
is quenched," he said. "In the desert you do not drink to
satisfy your throat. You drink to replenish the liquid the sun
sucks from the cells of your body. Thus you must learn to
change your appetite. Instead of drinking to enjoy, you drink
to live. It is far better to drink warm water that will go into your
entire system than to satisfy the desire of your throat and run
the risk of dehydration."

The same principle works in the spiritual area as well. The
manna of God was to be only temporary. Just a few days ahead
lay the Promised Land with milk, wine and honey. Only
further disobedience caused God to have to keep the manna
coming—for forty years.

The carnal appetite, which God was burning from them
with His prescribed diet, is never satisfied. It is like the throat
that has been tickled by carbonated soda water laced with
sugar. It always yearns for more. It causes men to run after
every new "prophet" who comes on the scene with a "new
revelation" from God. It causes men to trade the written Word
of God for the philosophy of man since it seems more palatable. It causes men to demand melons and meat while dis-
daining what God has placed before them.

But the only way to reach the Promised Land is by eating
God's diet. Leeks, onions and garlic will not get you into
Canaan, for that diet is always accompanied by the bondage of
Egypt. In the wilderness we must make priority decisions.
Are we willing to give up what satisfies the belly in order to
have what satisfies the soul?

Those who ignore or refuse God's provision while lusting
for the former things (which the Bible says must eventually be
"put away") will soon perish and be buried in the sands of the

wilderness—the very place where God's manna which they rejected so covered the earth.

Yet the others—those who accept God's meager diet on faith, believing God has a purpose for what He serves up— enter into a marvelous truth that lean diets are intended only for a season. To those who obey and do not grumble, there lies ahead a table in the wilderness. Here, then, is the truth: While we are in the wilderness, we are not of the wilderness. We are bound for a Promised Land.

VIII

Relationships

"It is an everlasting covenant of salt before the Lord for both you and your offspring."

(Numbers 18:19)

Those of us making our way through our personal wildernesses are forced, for the purpose of preservation, to huddle. At night when the rocks cool and the frigid winter wind whistles through the deep wadis, we gather in our tents to savor each other's warmth.

In the scorching heat of noonday, when the only shade is an overhanging rock, we build our booths of date palm branches to escape the deadly sun.

At the wells we huddle, sharing from the cups of our hands.

Those of us who have spent long periods in the Sinai realize quickly that there are few genuine habitable places in the wilderness. The wilderness is not a place to settle, only a place to pass through. But to live apart, even on a pilgrimage, invites death. Thus the wilderness forces us into relationships.

Often we are not aware of the intensity of these relationships until it is time to separate. Then, like children on the last night of a lengthy summer camp, or like soldiers gathering in the barracks the night before each returns to his home following the war, we grow nostalgic. After having been thrust together for the sake of survival, we often find we've done more than survive; we have begun to live.

I remember one of those "last nights" in particular. Our group of twelve men had gathered in a natural grotto, hewn by the hand of the wind over countless centuries. The sandstone walls of the cave provided scores of tiny alcoves where we placed candles. Then, settling on the soft white sand, we got quiet, praying, singing softly and simply sitting still. Our little "family," which had been together for two weeks, was at the end of the trail. The next day we would load up our Land Rover and head back along the Gulf of Aqaba, through Elat, northward through the Aravah to the Dead Sea, past Jericho and back to Jerusalem. There the "family" would dissolve, each of us flying back to wherever we came from to resume our busy schedules.

But while we had been in the Sinai we had grown close. We had entered into relationships. In this crucible, men who had been strangers had become friends for life, bound together by the commonness of our trek through tough times. Just having been there somehow made us brothers, pledged to a sacred fraternity of those who had also passed this way.

The wilderness breeds loyalty. It forces us into a camaraderie of deep covenant relationships.

In the Middle East, families still return for reunions at the time of harvest. Even though they no longer harvest the fields, they still remember the covenants of the past when it was necessary to work together or perish separately.

So it is with families who have been through hard times together, who have together suffered great losses. They are always closer than those children of opulence who have never had to struggle for food and shelter.

Thus it is not surprising that God chose the wilderness to reveal His covenant nature. Covenant in its purest form is a binding and solemn agreement between individuals who compact toward a common goal. It grows out of conflict and is always tested by suffering.

To Noah, staggered by the immensity of God's wrath, God covenanted: "I have set my rainbow in the clouds, and it will be the sign of the covenant" (Genesis 9:13).

To Abraham, wandering childless and without purpose in the desert, God covenanted: "This is my covenant with you: You will be the father of many nations" (Genesis 17:4).

Such were the covenants between God and man. But there were covenants between men of God as well. Of these, none is as strong and binding as the oldest of them all—the covenant of loyalty. It was birthed in the awesome grandeur of the desert between men to whom loyalty spelled the difference between life and death. It was called the Covenant of Salt.

There is no recorded time for its beginning. Indeed, it seems to be the oldest of all the covenants and was already in effect as a recognized pact when the children of Israel began their slow and torturous trek across the wilderness of the Sinai.

It is first mentioned in Numbers 18:19 as a sign to the priests in their offerings to the Lord. "Whatever is set aside from the holy offerings. . . . It is an everlasting covenant of salt before the Lord for both you and your offspring."

Later God told the Levites to season all grain offerings with salt. "Do not leave the salt of the covenant of your God out of your grain offerings; add salt to all your offerings" (Leviticus 2:13).

From the very earliest times salt was a symbol of the covenant.

To the Levites it was a sign of perpetual purity. But to the people it had a much broader meaning—a meaning preserved to this day among the people who live in the Sinai, those nomadic Bedouin whose history predates even the time of Moses.

The Bedouin have a lofty concept of the sanctity of women. Besides this, women play the role of shepherd. Since the flocks are the life sustenance of the tribe, and the shepherds are at the heart of the flock structure, it is necessary to protect the women. The law of the desert says if a man molests a woman, then the woman's husband or her brothers are free to go after the molester, track him down and kill him. Not only do they have jurisdiction over the life of the molester, but over the lives of his brothers as well, to prevent revenge. In the desert, a man is literally his brother's keeper, since his own life may depend on his brother's behavior.

As a result of this seemingly harsh but fair law, women go unmolested. They wear the traditional black dress with black facial veil that causes them to stand out against the white sand of the desert. No man can use the excuse of just "happening" upon a woman shepherd, for they can be spotted from a great distance. And the law of the desert says, "Stay clear."

Of course, this hampers the legitimate romantic inclinations of any man with honorable intentions. To approach a woman randomly, even for honorable reasons, is to invite trouble since she may accuse him of molesting her. Therefore, the Bedouin use an ancient but complicated procedure for romantic introduction.

The young man is never allowed to propose to a girl or, for that matter, even approach her outright. Rather, after watching her from afar as she tends her flock, the young man will wait until she has left the place where she watered her animals, and when night comes he will come to the well or spring. He will then put his footprint in the sand in a conspicuous place where she can see it the next day. When she returns to the watering spot, she sees his footprint. If she is interested in meeting him, she will place her footprint alongside his in the sand. Returning again after she has left, and seeing the two prints side-by-side in the sand, the young man knows the way is now open for the next step.

Even then he may not approach her. Nor does he even approach her father. Instead, he sends his brother or a friend to go and sit down and talk with the father. They will discuss many things, as Bedouin do. They will talk about the father's sheep and goats, about tribal situations, about relatives, about the weather. Finally the intermediary will get around to bringing up the subject of the father's daughter. After many compliments he will mention that his brother (or his friend) is interested in meeting the daughter and would like the father's permission. If the father indicates he approves of this relationship (rather than one he may have already picked out), he gives permission for the young man to come see him personally. Once done, he then gives permission to the young man to speak to his daughter.

After a period of time, if marriage is acceptable, the bridegroom brings many expensive gifts. The father of the bride then arranges a betrothal ceremony, which is as binding as marriage. This is followed, later on, by a three-day marriage ceremony accompanied by feasting and merriment, complete with camel races and festivities for family and friends who come from many miles.

Following the wedding, the bride returns to the tent of her mother and learns other things about married life. During this time, the groom will return to his place and make his winter tent, the heavy black tent of goat's hair and skins, to protect his bride from the harsh desert winters. When this task is completed, the groom places his tent near the tent of the bride's father and, in a final ceremony, comes to the family tent to claim his bride—a ceremony alluded to in the book of Revelation called "the marriage supper of the Lamb" when the Bridegroom (Christ) returns to claim His bride (the Church) who has been prepared "without spot or wrinkle."

An ancient Bedouin custom calls for the "circumcision" of infant girls to discourage indiscriminate sexual activity before marriage. This excising is done to prevent the sexual act from being pleasurable and thus to protect the girl's virginity—which is promised by the bride's father to the bridegroom as part of the marriage contract. (Only the Jebeliya tribe, located in the vicinity of St. Catherine's Monastery—who were once Christian but became Moslem—do not excise the baby girls.)

To determine the virgin state of the bride, the bridegroom places a white ceremonial sheet on the ground beneath the bride on her nuptial night. This sheet is then shown to the bride's father the next morning. The presence of a spot of blood is proof of virginity, and a sign the marriage covenant is valid. Its absence is valid reason for divorce. The bridegroom is then allowed to reclaim all the gifts that he gave the bride's father.

If the marriage is happily consummated, the young couple join the household of the bride's father and continue to tend the flocks of the father-in-law into the future.

During the process of the marriage ceremony, which is conducted by the tribal sheikh (priest, head elder), the covenant of salt takes place. Sometimes salt is sprinkled upon the joined hands of the bridal couple. Other times it is sprinkled on their heads.

Salt is a sign of precious and sacred covenant, for covenants are never entered into without a sign. Each time God entered into a covenant with man, there was a sign. With Noah, it was a rainbow in the sky. With Abraham, it was accompanied by circumcision. With Moses, it was the tablets of stone. Later, heaps of stones were often set up as memorials. The sacrificial offerings were a continuing sign of the covenant.

In Jesus' story of the return of the Prodigal Son, the killing of the fatted calf was more than a celebration: it was a sign of a covenant between father and son. When John the Baptist pointed to Jesus on the banks of the Jordan River and proclaimed, "Look, the Lamb of God, who takes away the sin of the world," he was referring to a new covenant—a sign fulfilled literally in the Eucharist when Jesus said, "This cup is the new covenant in my blood."

To the Bedouin, salt was (and is) of great value in the desert. In fact, the legend goes, in early times blocks of salt were part of the dowry of the young woman preparing for marriage—as valuable in the desert as gold on the stock market.

In common life, salt was a symbol of covenant relationships. Salt contained the power to strengthen food and preserve it from putrefaction and corruption. In the sacrifice this meant the unbending truthfulness and loyalty between God and man. Thus it was commanded that the Levites present salt in the grain offering and add it to all the other offerings as a sign of continued loyalty and purification.

It is stated that, in the time of David, his kingdom was established by a covenant of salt—a covenant that was for him and his descendants forever. "Ought ye not to know that the Lord God of Israel gave the kingdom over Israel to David for ever, even to him and to his sons by a covenant of salt?" (II Chronicles 13:5, KJV).

Salt represented covenant relationships. Even in the desert today when Arab men get together, they may express their loyalty and devotion to one another by saying, "There is salt between us."

When Jesus told His disciples, "Ye are the salt of the earth," He was speaking of this covenant of loyalty. Many of us have heard sermons on that passage from the Sermon on the Mount, pointing out how salt preserves, purifies, seasons, even creates thirst. All are true points. But they are merely incidental to the central theme of the biblical concept of salt, for salt represents covenant. It represents covenant between men, and between men and God.

Salt means loyalty. When Jesus emphasized the imperativeness of saltiness, He was referring to the necessity of walking out the covenant with God and with one another. Such covenants are forged and consummated in the crucible of wilderness experiences.

Covenant people are people who have come through the fire together. They are people loyal to one another. They are people who will die for each other. They are people who refuse to entertain malicious charges against each other. They are people who love one another, who serve one another, who do not need to swear to one another because their word is their bond. They are people of one family.

Shakespeare understood this when he had old Polonius advise Laertes in *Hamlet* with these words:

> Be thou familiar, but by no means vulgar.
> The friends thou hast, and their adoption
>   tried,
> Grapple them to thy soul with hoops of steel;
> But do not dull thy palm with entertainment
> Of each new-hatched, unfledged comrade.

Covenant friends are friends tried in the wilderness. When one finds such a friend, he should be grappled to one's soul with hoops of steel.

Leonardo da Vinci caught this concept in his painting of the Last Supper. All the men sitting at the table with Jesus were men of loyalty—all save one. On the table in front of Judas was an upended salt shaker, its contents spilling onto the cloth. It was the perfect symbol of broken covenant.

We live in an age of easiness. We do our best to keep away from hardship. Even family discipline is legislated against by government bodies. Covenants no longer exist. Contracts are easily dissolved. Divorce is easier than marriage. Children are free to leave their parents. Parents desert children and brag about it. Churches, which are supposed to be spiritual families, often split over issues of ego. Arabs and Jews, coming from the same stock, attempt to eliminate each other from the earth.

Men and women who have walked through the wilderness together, on the other hand, form binding relationships that are never broken. Here covenants are formed. They are tested until proven secure.

Such loyalty forms a kind of cloth, tightly woven with threads of love and trust. This cloth covers each other's faults from the eyes of a cruel world. It bandages each other's wounds, and becomes a banner that leads us together toward a land of promise.

So it is with the covenant of salt—the perfect symbol of the wilderness compact. Salt is composed of two elements that, if taken separately, are poison: sodium and chlorine. Either will kill instantly. But mixed together, these two elements form an ingredient absolutely essential to life.

The wilderness experienced by itself kills. But the wilderness experienced with others brews a recipe of hardy nourishment.

Such is the covenant of salt.

IX

Pilgrims

In all the travels of the Israelites, whenever the cloud lifted from above the tabernacle, they would set out; but if the cloud did not lift, they did not set out—until the day it lifted.

(Exodus 40:36-37)

There are three kinds of people in the wilderness. The hermits move in from the outside, settle in caves and stay in one place until they die. The Bedouin are nomads, on the move but always in a circle. However, God never intends for His children to settle in the wilderness as hermits or nomads. We are thus to be the third breed of wilderness person—the pilgrim. Each wilderness experience becomes a pilgrimage—an experience in which we meet, know and follow God to His land of promise.

The process is simple, although often painful.

The chemist of the Holy Spirit takes the elements of our lives and drops them into the mortar of the wilderness setting. Then, using circumstances as a pestle, He crushes our natural elements until they come into union with each other. Pouring that fine dust into a crucible, He turns up the heat until all the impurities burst into tiny flames and disappear, leaving behind the purified self, perfectly integrated, ready for service—working all things together for good.

This is never a static process. It always involves change and progress from one stage to another. It can be done only on the move.

To some degree, all life on earth is a wilderness experience. As surely as sparks fly upward, Job pointed out, we are born into trouble. But the wilderness is a passage through trouble, not a place to stop and wallow in our adversity. As the old Negro spiritual says: "This world is not my home, I'm just a-passing through."

Every road sign on our trek through the wilderness of this mortal life points toward a glorious consummation of life eternal with God. We are not born to die; we are born to be reborn—and live forever. As we move toward that heavenly experience, which awaits all the saints, we pass through trouble, adversity, grief, pain and hardships—all wilderness experiences. But these deserts are not designed to choke the life from us; rather, they are designed to mold us and shape us into the image of Christ. We are not ever to allow ourselves to become desert settlers like the hermits of old, or even the Bedouin of today. We are pilgrims, "a-passing through."

God knew how easy it would be for these former slaves who had never been anywhere to settle for another Egypt. The first order of business, therefore, as a father keeps a freezing child walking to keep him alive, was to keep the children of Israel on the move. Stopping, especially if they stopped without purpose, would allow them to begin thinking of the fleshpots of Egypt, or to grow lazy and inert and settle for second-best, rather than move on to the Promised Land.

At Marah they stopped, grumbled and resigned themselves to die in the desert. At Sinai they stopped, grumbled and finally built a golden calf to occupy their time and worship. At Kadesh-Barnea, where they spent 38 years, they grew tired of manna, grumbled and cried out to return to Egypt. At Kadesh-Barnea they voted to settle in the desert rather than occupy the Promised Land. Every time they stopped, it seemed, they grew lethargic and dissatisfied.

To keep them up and moving, God placed a cloud over the tabernacle by day and a pillar of fire by night.

The cloud, which glowed with fire during the night, was placed over the tabernacle itself—the tent of meeting that contained the Ark of the Covenant. As long as the cloud was stationary, the people remained in that place. When the cloud moved, they folded their tents, dismantled the tabernacle, packed all their belongings and moved out under the cloud. According to the Book of Numbers, sometimes the cloud remained stationary only a few days at a time. Sometimes the cloud stayed only from evening till morning. At other times it remained over the tabernacle for months or a year at a time. But "at the Lord's command they encamped, and at the Lord's command they set out" (Numbers 9:23).

It is an ancient and valid military procedure to train men until they react to orders instinctively. The manual of arms, even though it is never used in war, is a training procedure, teaching soldiers to react to an order instinctively without arguing. A good soldier never asks why. He simply does his job, believing there is purpose behind the order which he does not understand, but which a superior military intellect does understand. As Kipling had his Light Brigade say: "Ours not to question why, ours but to do and die. . . ."

But there was an even greater purpose in keeping the Hebrews moving. God wanted them to keep their eyes on Him. Hermits—those who live in caves and spend their lives contemplating—tend to become self-conscious rather than others-conscious. But the purpose of any wilderness is to force us to get our eyes off ourselves, off our problems, off the circumstances—to enter into family relationships where God is Father. The placement of the cloud demanded this. It covered the entire nation of people. If the children of Israel were ever to leave this "great and terrible wilderness," it would have to be under God's direction and protection, and as a group.

Every morning, therefore, they were forced to leave their tents and look up to see if the cloud had moved. Even after they reached Kadesh-Barnea, the cloud remained. On occasion it moved just slightly, perhaps just over the next sand dune. Since the Israelites were placed in position around the tabernacle, with each tribe occupying a certain sector, any movement of the tabernacle meant the entire camp had to move. Therefore, whether they moved ten miles or only 200 yards, it still meant pulling up all the tent pegs, folding their tents, and moving to another location.

Dissatisfaction with God's plan was invariably accompanied by grumbling. Time after time God demanded that the children of Israel stop their grumbling and fasten their eyes on Him, rather than look always at the less-than-perfect circumstances. In fact, it seems God deliberately allowed some of these adverse circumstances just so the children of Israel would be forced to look to Him—or perish.

Perhaps the most dramatic event occurred after the Israelites left Kadesh-Barnea and were marching slowly toward Edom on their way to Canaan. Once again the people grew impatient with God. "They spoke against God and against Moses, and said, 'Why have you brought us up out of Egypt to die in the desert? There is no bread! There is no water! And we detest this miserable food!'" (Numbers 21:5).

It was a complaint God had heard many times from these people. To teach them a lesson, "the Lord sent venomous snakes among them; they bit the people and many Israelites died" (verse 6).

Immediately the people repented and came crying to Moses, saying, "We sinned when we spoke against the Lord and against you. Pray that the Lord will take the snakes away from us" (verse 7).

But instead of removing the snakes, God taught them a lesson. He taught them to look to Him, rather than at the circumstances. The Lord told Moses to make a bronze snake and put it on a pole. "Anyone who is bitten can look at it and live," God said (verse 8).

Twelve hundred years later Jesus, speaking to an expert in Jewish history, reminded him of this experience. He had just told Nicodemus that natural birth does not qualify a man to enter the Kingdom of heaven; he needs to be born again of the Spirit. When Nicodemus questioned him, Jesus said, "Just as Moses lifted up the snake in the desert, so the Son of Man must be lifted up, that everyone who believes in him may have eternal life" (John 3:14-15).

In both instances God was saying, "It is not enough to lean to your own understanding. Life is found only when you trust Me to direct your paths."

The poison vipers still live in the desert. One afternoon a small group of us were driving through a mile-wide wadi south of Mt. Sinai when our six-wheel-drive truck hit a rock and destroyed a tire. It was the fourth tire we had destroyed in two days. It was going to take several hours for our driver to pull the tire from the rim, patch the tube and replace the tire.

While this was going on, four of us headed for the only shade within a mile—a spiny acacia tree growing in the middle of the wadi. I was standing next to one of the men under the tree when I looked down. There, half-buried in the sand at the base of the tree, only inches from my friend's open-toed sandal, was a deadly carpet viper, coiled to strike.

I silently motioned the other men to step back. With my hand on my friend's shoulder, I directed his eyes to his feet. We had been warned of the carpet viper. This one, gray and green in color, had already raised its head—beady eyes staring, forked tongue darting in and out. Belonging to the cobra family, its venom attacks the central nervous system, bringing agonizing death in less than ten minutes.

Gradually we moved backwards, away from the swaying head of the three-foot snake. Once at a safe distance, we found large stones and killed the snake. "You are very fortunate," our guide said solemnly. "Only God could have saved you had you been bitten."

It was that concept that the Lord was trying to implant in the hearts of the Israelites. Much earlier He had said, "I am the Lord who heals you." Thirty-eight years later, He demonstrated that truth when He told the people to look to Him when they were bitten. It was a lesson all pilgrims must learn—or die.

The only time a wilderness experience becomes a tragedy is when we fail to understand that the purpose of adversity is to force us to look to God. The wilderness is a school. While there are those who seem to be professional students—always sitting at a desk like overgrown oafs, finding it safer to attend school than earn a living—God's purpose for us is to graduate and become self-supporting.

When we understand we are enrolled in "the school of the wilderness" for a season only, and shall eventually "pass through to the other side," we cannot only exist, we can even enjoy the passage. But if we grow discouraged, if we grow spiritually lazy and linger behind, if we get our eyes off the goal of the Promised Land and become enamored of the wilderness itself, we will surely die.

The true pilgrim never stops to build monuments in the wilderness. At best, he may leave road signs pointing the way for the next group of pilgrims. But if he remains behind when the cloud moves, he will never have the desire or initiative to catch up.

The mark of identity of the Israelites was not their common slavehood of the past. The mark of identity was the fact they were all pilgrims, under the leadership of God who was "on the move."

"Unless you go with us . . . what will distinguish your people from all the other people on the face of the earth?" Moses asked God. They were pilgrims, moving through the wilderness, led by God.

It is interesting that today's archaeologists have been unable to discover a single shred of archaeological evidence in the Sinai to substantiate the Exodus. There are records on stone or buried in the ground of all the people who lived in the Sinai, before and after the Exodus. The Amalekites, the Hyksos, the Egyptians, the Nabateans—all left their marks. Archaeologists digging in the sand have been able to identify civilizations dating all the way back to the Early Bronze Age five thousand years ago. In fact, traces of Early Bronze Age domestic ruins and pottery shards at Wadi esh Sheikh in south-central Sinai indicate a large settlement there.

But there is absolutely no record of the Israelites. There are no rock carvings, no signs of permanent buildings, not even any pottery shards. The reason? The Israelites were a people on the move. Pilgrims. As the Jews today, they were a neat people. They did not leave their garbage behind. They were a busy people with no time to stop and chip graffiti on the walls of canyons. Despite their grumblings and complainings, they had a goal. They were a people under leadership, moving from slavery to freedom. Thus it is silent proof of the authenticity of the biblical account that no archaeological evidence has been found—for pilgrims seldom leave anything behind.

Following the cloud meant the Israelites had to keep their lives simple. They could not become too comfortable because any day they could awake and find the cloud had moved over the next sand dune, down the wadi, to the next mountaintop. How easy it is to miss God's direction by investing too much in material things, by giving too much emphasis to our earthly place. Leaving it, then, becomes a wrenching experience. Nothing is as sad as the man who has heard the call of God, but could not go because he has pledged his soul to the finance company.

Peter Marshall put it well in one of his famous prayers before the U.S. Senate:

> Forbid it, Lord, that our roots become too firmly attached to this earth, that we should fall in love with things. Help us to understand that the pilgrimage of this life is but an introduction, a preface, a training school for what is to come. . . .

Life is designed by God as a pilgrimage composed of many wildernesses. God is forever saying to all of us, Travel light. Do not stop to build monuments. Do not overload yourself with sentimental memorabilia that ties the heartstrings to things of the past. Do not stake out sections of land as "sacred" and declare you can never leave them behind. If you have precious belongings, send them ahead. For as Jesus said, "Where your treasure is, there is your heart also."

I still shudder when I recall the half-sneer, half-laugh from the Jewish archaeologist when I asked about Jewish shrines. "We Jews do not build shrines," she said. "Only Christians stop to do that. We worship a God who is on the move."

It is significant to note that the Jews never returned to build a shrine on Mt. Sinai, nor on the banks of the Sea of Reeds. Their allegiance was to a God symbolized by the mobile tabernacle and the Ark of the Covenant that preceded the column as it moved.

It is one of the important lessons of the desert: Keep moving! The pilgrim who pauses too long in any one place dies. Even the Bedouin, who seem bound like Prometheus to the rock of their wilderness wanderings, realize they must keep on the move. The Bedouin, though, are not pilgrims. They are nomads, wandering with the seasons in circles, with no Promised Land to beckon them onward. They are the prototype of spiritual squatters who camp smugly at certain points of tradition or doctrine—while the wind of God's Spirit blows past.

This is the story of the hermits who fled to the Sinai during the fourth and fifth centuries. Monks, recluses, they moved out of the mainstream of life—and never returned. Mistakenly they thought the cloud had come to rest over them, permanently.

During the years following the reign of the Roman emperor Constantine, who made Christianity acceptable (indeed, in many instances, made it mandatory), the Sinai became a haven for men looking for inner peace. From the naked hills of the Judean desert down through the Negev to the southern tip of the Sinai Peninsula, one still finds hermits' caves wherever there is spring water.

The word *hermit* came from the Greek word for desert, *eremia*. The desert and hermitry were inseparable in the Byzantine mind. For the hermit, God could be found only in the cruelest extremes. They abandoned their pagan world to seek, according to Catholic scholar Thomas Merton, salvation. They regarded society as a shipwreck from which each single individual had to swim for his life. Their only escape was the desert in which the impurities and dross of society could be burned and purged from their minds and hearts and bodies.

Some of them lived out their lives in total silence, even clipping their tongues so they could not speak even if tempted. Chains, near-starvation, self-flagellation and long exposure to unbearable elements were the usual course of life for these strange men who, fleeing this world, settled in a wilderness that God had long since left behind.

Their pilgrimage, as they saw it, was inner. They came to stay in order to take an inward journey to personal salvation. But in the process they stagnated. Instead of becoming servants, they became dependent upon others more practical and utilitarian to serve them. Eventually—like the Dead Sea which receives but never gives—some became mad parasites and died. And while a few did indeed come face-to-face with God, most hermits remain tragic examples in history of pilgrims who viewed the cloud as stationary.

We must learn a lesson from the hermits, though it be a negative one. Man is never called to enter a wilderness to find God, which is the essence of religion. Rather, when circumstances force us into a wilderness, we should have faith to believe God will take the initiative and reveal Himself to us in His time and place. Our responsibility is to respond, and stay under the cloud as it moves to God's destined purpose for our lives.

To view the wilderness as an end—a place of abiding, rather than a place through which one passes on his way to a land of promise—is the greatest of tragedies. Since God never intended that His children enter a wilderness and remain, each wilderness experience should be accompanied by a sense of nagging dissatisfaction, a deep longing for the Promised Land to come. Pilgrims should be careful not to try to escape the suffering God places on His children, until the object of that suffering is complete. At the same time, they should arise every morning and look upward—expecting, yea *knowing*, that one day the cloud will move.

Depression, discouragement, unhappiness, feelings of unworthiness—all these are moods of the wilderness. But the promise of God is far greater and can be experienced long before one actually emerges from the wilderness. Therefore, it is not unusual to hear, even from wilderness beds, songs in the night.

Even though the reed is bruised He will not break it off. Even though the wick is only smoldering He will not snuff it out. While each desert is a place of burning, the promise of God remains: "When you walk through the fire, you will not be burned; the flames will not set you ablaze" (Isaiah 43:2).

X

Obedience

"Strike the rock, and water will come out of it for the people to drink."

(Exodus 17:6)

Few desert experiences are as welcome—or as terrifying—as rain. Especially is this true in the high mountain regions of the Sinai.

Average rainfall in the southern Sinai is less than three inches per year. There are no rivers, no lakes, no forests, no meadows—just bare rock, boulders and sand, with only a few plants adapted to these harsh conditions. Rain rarely falls, but when it does, it is torrential. In fact, the desert may go for years without any rain, then have it all fall at one time.

My first encounter with rain in the Sinai was an awesome experience. Our small group had made camp early in a narrow part of Wadi Nasb. It was an ideal place to spend the night. The almost sheer granite walls of the canyon extended upward from the soft white sand of the wadi floor. The narrow, twisting pass provided a sense of ultimate privacy as we unloaded our sleeping gear from the truck and set up the butane tanks so we could heat water for our evening meal.

All day long we had noticed a rare buildup of clouds to the southwest, over the St. Catherine range near Mt. Sinai. The clouds were miles away, however, and we did not expect it would rain on us during the night—although there was a strong possibility it had been raining in the high mountains.

I had gone up the wadi several hundred yards to find an "alone place" to spread my sleeping bag for the night when I noticed the sand under my feet was moist. I had been in this area a number of times and knew there were no springs. Why then this moisture, when overhead it was clear?

Instead of unrolling my sleeping bag, I returned to the truck and told our guide what I had discovered.

"It's time to move to higher ground," he said. "This wadi may be getting ready to fill up with water."

We quickly called the men together, reloaded the truck and headed back down the wadi. By the time we reached a wider place where we could pull the truck onto a high plateau, the water was already beginning to flow down this ancient waterway. The rain in the high mountains, although miles from where we were, had cascaded off the sides of the granite mountains in great sheets. Like waterfalls, it had flooded the narrow wadis. Growing in size, the raging river was surging toward the sea through the waterways that empty in this region near Dahab. This has happened for centuries, causing a huge alluvial plain that fans out from the coast into the Gulf of Aqaba.

From our new high perch we watched the wadi, where only minutes before we had been spreading our sleeping bags, become a raging, torrential river. The muddy water came pouring out of the mouth of the wadi in an awesome eruption. Within minutes it was no longer a trickling stream, but a mighty cataract almost twelve feet deep, sweeping along everything that lay in its path. Trees were uprooted and huge boulders tumbled along as wood chips in the current. I sat watching, amazed, fascinated at the power of the eruption.

The year before a similar flood had swept down out of the high mountains toward the south, roaring through the wadis and erupting at Sharm el Sheikh, filling the hotel up to the second floor with water and sand before emptying into the Red Sea. That particular flood had swept away two Bedouin villages, killing three children. On another occasion, just a few months prior, a similar flashflood had poured out of the Negev Desert near Ein Gedi, washing away the main highway from Jericho to Eilat and sweeping a pickup truck with three teenagers into the Dead Sea, where all perished.

Sitting on my rocky perch high above the raging torrent, I gave thanks we had not been caught in that narrow wadi at night, resting in our sleeping bags when the water from the high mountains surged through. Then we waited for the water to go down, which took about an hour, and then made our way to another area where we spent the night on dry sand. The next morning, after the sun was up and the desert exposed to the heat and wind, the ground was once again parched and dry. We continued our way up Wadi Nasb to our destination.

During these occasional flashfloods an extraordinary event may take place. As the wall of water rages through the wadis, sometimes as deep as thirty feet, it exerts great force on the walls of the canyons. At the places where igneous and sedimentary rocks come together in the sides of the mountains, the water occasionally hollows out great fissures inside the mountains. These hollow mountains become literal reservoirs, holding sometimes thousands of gallons, forced into them by the floods.

After the flood has passed, the water begins to seep from its mountain reservoir. Calcium deposits quickly form around the opening, sealing off the water in the rock. When the winter snows melt, this moisture percolates into the ground and replenishes these reservoirs. Sometimes this water will be absorbed into the ground and reappear farther down the wadi as a spring. At other times it remains trapped in the rock.

I have watched a Bedouin shepherd, in an action called a *t'mile*, take his heavy staff and, by striking the rock at exactly the right point, break loose the blockage, allowing the water to gush forth. It was this action Moses took when faced with another water emergency.

Continuing their trek inland toward the high mountains, the Israelites noticed how the scenery began to change. The burning sand gave way to massive granite mountains. These were crossed by numerous dykes, flows of magma that had forced their way up along fissures in the rocks from earlier volcanic action. The colors changed, too, from gray and yellow sand to the mixture of rock displays in various shades of red, pink, black and purple, crossed by the dykes with streaks of dark green, black and crimson. There was no vegetation, no skin to cover this skeleton of the countryside. The people walked silently as their leader marched through the narrow canyons and around steep bends where minute by minute the scenery changed before their eyes, forbidding and breathtaking.

To each of the Israelites the mountains had a different meaning. To some they looked like the work of a master mason; to others like a host of bowed and petrified giants. Still others felt they were looking at a battlefield abandoned by giants who had been hurling great stones at each other. Whatever the feeling, each one sensed he was entering an area that was sacred, holy, set apart.

Before them, in the distant southeast, they could catch glimpses of the sun reflecting off the towering peak of Mt. Sinai. To get there, they would have to go through Watia Pass, a deep cleft in a peculiar wall-like body of granite that looked like the work of a sword-wielding giant who had slashed the landscape in frustrated anger. Beyond the pass the landscape changed, the mountains becoming even wilder, higher and more barren. How could they survive? Where, here in these high, desolate mountains, could they find water?

Therefore, despite feelings of awe, the grumbling began once again. "The whole Israelite community set out from the Desert of Sin, traveling from place to place as the Lord commanded. They camped at Rephidim, but there was no water for the people to drink. So they quarreled with Moses and said, 'Give us water to drink'" (Exodus 17:1-2).

Moses rebuked the people, saying they were doubting God's ability to take care of them. But thirst drives people into panic. As they murmured at the springs of Marah, so they did at Rephidim. "Why did you bring us up out of Egypt to make us and our children and livestock die of thirst?" (Exodus 17:3).

Exasperated, Moses cried out to God for help. Then, deep in his spirit, he remembered this place. The presence of the dykes, the mixture of sandstone and granite—surely there would be a water reservoir behind one of these rock walls.

Moving ahead of the people with some of the older tribal leaders, he walked slowly up the wadi, gently tapping the rock walls with his staff. Suddenly there was a soft spot. Commanding the people to fetch their water containers, he drew back his staff and with a mighty blow smashed his heavy rod into the calcium deposit on the side of the mountain.

Instantly it broke, and water gushed forth.

It was really not necessary, for just a mile or so beyond that place lay the richest, lushest oasis in the Sinai. Moses could have commanded the people to stop their murmuring, put them in a forced march, and reached the oasis in Wadi Feiran within the hour. But God wanted to reveal His miraculous power through Moses. Even though the *t'mile* was something Moses had done before at different places in the Sinai, this was a new occurrence for the Israelites. The people were on the verge of losing respect for their leader. On the morrow, another event (which will be covered in the next chapter) was to take place, one that would change the course of their lives, and the direction of their leader's life as well. Therefore, even though God could have directed Moses to keep moving to the natural springs just ahead, He chose instead to let Moses get the glory in the eyes of the people by striking the rock.

It would be another forty years before Moses was faced with a similar challenge. It happened in the vicinity of Kadesh-Barnea about the time the wilderness wanderings were over. The exact time and place remain unknown. Preparation was almost complete for them to move northward to possess the land. Once again, though, the Israelites were without water.

As he had done years before near Rephidim, Moses approached the Lord. "Take the staff, and you and your brother Aaron gather the assembly together. Speak to that rock before their eyes and it will pour out its water. You will bring water out of the rock for the community so they and their livestock can drink" (Numbers 20:8).

But a subtle change had taken place in Moses over the years. Earlier in his life he had been a man who listened keenly and adjusted immediately. He had been a man of daring, venturesome faith. But Moses had grown old. His ways were set. He no longer welcomed change but resisted it by fleeing to the safe harbor of tradition. He was like Tevye in Sholem Aleichem's *Fiddler on the Roof*. "How do we keep our balance?" the old Jew asked. "I can tell you in one word: tradition. . . .

Without our traditions our lives would be as shaky as a fiddler on the roof."

Moses was no longer willing to dance to God's tune. The roof was too steep. The danger of falling too great. He had slipped into a trap many wilderness pilgrims mire in—the trap of tradition. He failed to remember how many tombstones dotted the desert with the epitaph *We've Never Done It This Way Before*.

True, there is protection in tradition. It eliminates unnecessary risk; it prevents our making the same mistake twice. Tradition takes the fiddler from the roof and places him on solid ground—perhaps even locks him in the basement of the church. But there is a vast difference between learning from history and becoming a slave to dead tradition. There is safety in tradition, but it often keeps one from hearing the voice of God. Equally tragic, tradition may bind the one who does hear that voice.

Moses was no longer a new wineskin. He had become old. His wineskin was dry and cracked. His spirit, although still faithful to God, had lost its elasticity. He no longer had the willingness to expand. It was easier to do it as he had done it in the past—successfully, I may add—than to venture out and attempt something new, even though God had commanded it.

Thus, instead of speaking to the rock as God had commanded, Moses reverted to a time-tested procedure. He struck the rock in a *t'mile* as he had done so many years before at Rephidim. Not only that, but he struck it with bitterness and arrogance. "Listen, you rebels," he shouted, "must we bring you water out of this rock?" (Numbers 20:10).

Water came forth, of course. Humanistic knowledge, too, produces results. But even though Moses brought forth water, he did it in his own strength. Many years later, as the Jews were rebuilding the Temple under Zerubbabel, God again spoke of this single aspect of His character: He demands absolute obedience by leaders, and He will not share the glory with any man. The work of the Lord must not be done by human cunning or strength. "'Not by might nor by power, but by my Spirit,' says the Lord Almighty" (Zechariah 4:6).

Therefore, even though Moses got results—and the people

were pleased—another truth was evident: *God is not as inter-ested in ends as He is in means.* In fact, how we do a thing seems more important to God than whether we succeed. The means are not only more important than the end; the means are an end themselves. It was a truth Jesus also taught: God does not require men to succeed, He just requires them to be faithful.

Earlier, at Rephidim, God had pushed Moses to front stage. He wanted the people to hear him, to respect him, to follow him. But this was a new generation. These young men and women were learning there was more to being under authori-ty than following a powerful, knowledgeable, charismatic leader who knew how to get water out of a rock. They were learning to hear the voice of God for themselves. And that is always done best by following the example of their leader—a leader who had just proved himself unable.

It is a sad commentary on many of us. We begin so well and finish so poorly—not because we sin but because we get careless, because we lose that fine edge of faith, because we find it easier to drive in the ruts than to strike out over new territory.

Moses was like the Jewish driver of our desert vehicle who refused to leave the ruts in one of the wide wadis. I had asked him to pull out of the ruts made by a previous truck many months before so we could explore an abandoned turquoise mine.

"Too dangerous," he grunted. He then went on to explain how the Egyptians had placed explosive landmines in this particular wadi during the Six-Day War. They had then fled, but before the Israelis could clear the mines, a flashflood had roared through the wadi, scattering the mines for miles down the old riverbed. The only safe place to drive was in the ruts. In fact, the driver told me, just a few months before an Israeli colonel had been killed when his jeep ran over one of those old landmines and it exploded.

I understood his point. But staying in the ruts would mean we could never explore the unknown. "Just walk lightly," he said, slouching down in his seat and pulling his cap over his eyes for a nap. "I'll be waiting here—if you get back."

We did get back, our pockets full of bright green and aqua turquoise nuggets. The driver examined our treasures, then reminded us it was "Tradition!" that had kept the Jews alive all these centuries. "But," he chuckled, "we don't have any turquoise either."

Ruts are safe and comfortable. But the primary lesson of the wilderness is to bring us to the place where we can hear God and walk in His ways—even when He says to get out of the ruts.

Moses had lost his willingness to change. It was a sad day, for that meant he was disqualified to lead the young Israelites into Canaan. But the nation of Israel needed a leader who could obey orders. At the *Yam Suph*, Moses held out his rod and the wind blew back the water. But soon, in just a few months, this new generation would be approaching another watery barrier. The Jordan would be at flood stage. And instead of placing a man at the edge of the water, God had a deeper intention for this emerging nation. God wanted them to exhibit faith. They were to march into the water as it swirled around their feet. Only then would the water recede—not at the voice of a leader, but at the faith of men of God marching forward into a new world. If Moses could not obey God at the rock at Kadesh-Barnea, what would he do at the Jordan? Or, even more critical, how would he respond to the illogical instructions at the seige of Jericho? The wilderness lessons are stark.

What worked yesterday is not sufficient for today.

God's word yesterday must be adjusted by God's word today.

To be tyrannized by the past is the worst of all tyrannies.

The rut of tradition is but one step removed from a grave in the wilderness.

God's word to His pilgrims is fresh every morning. It is a lamp to our feet and a light to our path. Even though it may run counter to our traditions, or seem foolish at times, the man who trusts in Him will never be embarrassed or defeated.

> I will instruct you and teach you in the way
>   you should go;
> I will counsel you and watch over you.
> Do not be like the horse or the mule,
>   which have no understanding

but must be controlled by bit and bridle
or they will not come to you.
Many are the woes of the wicked,
but the Lord's unfailing love
surrounds the man who trusts in him.

(Psalm 32:8-10)

XI

Faith

Moses built an altar and called it The Lord is my Banner. He said, "For hands were lifted up to the throne of the Lord."
(Exodus 17:15-16)

As the Israelites moved deeper into the Sinai, the faith of Moses was evidenced again and again. But no place was it enunciated more clearly than when the Israelites arrived at Rephidim and were attacked by the fierce army of Amalek.

I have walked that same path toward Wadi Feiran where we find ancient Rephidim. The Israelites were weary from their journey, and the older and more infirm were straggling behind as the slow-moving procession made its tedious climb upward through Wadi Feiran toward the high mountain area. A little over halfway between Suez and Mt. Sinai, near the base of Jebel Serabal, is the most beautiful oasis in the Sinai. A number of springs feed an underground river that flows on a rock base just beneath the surface of the shallow sand. Thousands of date palms fill the narrow wadi, which changes suddenly from dry desert to lush oasis at the elevation of 1,500 feet above sea level.

Although the high walls of the wadi seem to shut off the outside world, because of the presence of abundant water there is also abundant life. Camping there at night, I am always aware of the abundance of animal life. Jackals howl at night, and on several occasions, having spent the night on the sand near the base of an overhanging cliff, I have awakened to find leopard tracks near my sleeping bag. Here the voice of the bulbul is heard. But the sound most precious to the weary pilgrim overrides all others—the constant trickle of water.

This beautiful oasis extends for miles through Wadi Feiran. Groves of palms, tamarisks and olive trees provide shade and food. Bundles of luscious grapes dangle from green vineyards. Orange and grapefruit trees, planted by the Bedouin, provide fresh juice. As the wadi narrows at Rephidim, the mountains on both sides grow taller and the walls of the wadi steeper. They form a tumbled mass of color and shape. White boulders, walls of pink porphyry provide clefts from which herbs and flowers seem to spring. Towering red mountains contrast with the deep green of the waving palms. All provide a place of tranquillity and rest.

Wadi Feiran is now the home of many Bedouin who have gathered around the abundant water supply. But in Moses' time it was the dwelling place of the fierce Amalekites—the cave-dwellers.

According to Genesis 36:12, Amalek was a grandchild of Esau—Jacob's brother. But while Moses seems to have inherited Jacob's character (remember Jacob's name was later changed to *Israel*, which means "one who wrestled with God and lost"), the Amalekites remained, as their ancient forefather Esau, angry. These children of Esau have continued in their hatred against Israel whom they feel cheated them of their birthright. The confrontation between these two distant cousins at Rephidim marked perhaps the first conflict in history between Arab and Jew.

In Deuteronomy Moses reminded the Israelites just how treacherous these ancient terrorists were. "When you were weary and worn out, they met you on your journey and cut off all who were lagging behind; they had no fear of God" (Deuteronomy 25:18).

It was a wicked deed, slaughtering the old people and the children, the pregnant women and the sick who could not move quite as fast as the rest of the procession. Attacking at night as the straggling band of Jews made their way wearily toward the springs ahead, the Amalekites hit and ran. They knew nothing of the hospitality of their Bedouin cousins who offered food, water and shade to these pilgrims. They instead represented the enemies of God. As Moses said, "They had no fear of God."

There are, I believe, two kinds of people on earth. There are those who wrestle with God hoping to lose. Although some may say they always want to do the will of God, all mankind is still struggling with Him. The first group, however, honors Him in the struggle and does not want to bring harm to His cause or His people. Then there are those who are the "enemies of God." Their sole purpose is the elimination of all who call upon the name of Jehovah.

The Amalekites were such a people. They represented, however, more than a warring tribe composed of the descendants of Amalek. They represented that entire breed of people who are enemies of God and enemies of God's people. Like the serpent that strikes anything close by, the Amalekites did not need to be provoked to attack. The mere presence of God's people near their lair was all the justification they needed to kill. They had no regard for the sanctity of human life, no morals, no sense of ethics. Their sole purpose was to drive the Israelites into the sea. They were, to a real degree, the forerunners of all those nations in the Middle East who even today maintain an identical purpose.

The prophet Balaam described the Amalekites as "the first fruits of the heathen," or the beginning of all those races of people hostile toward the people of God. The contest between Amalek and the Israelites, therefore, takes on an ominous overtone when viewed as the foreshadow of the conflicts to follow, for the battle at Rephidim was the first attack of the kingdoms of this world against the Kingdom of God.

Moses understood this. He realized this battle represented a spiritual attack against the Kingdom of God. Thus he wisely chose to fight the battle both in "the heavenlies" and on earth.

Up until this point in history, Moses had been both leader and overseer, pastor and apostle, prophet and priest. At Rephidim his role as leader began to change. He was now 81 years old and, although still healthy and strong, realized the call on his life had broadened from that of being a line officer to that of a field general. From this point on, Moses gradually emerged not as the physical leader of Israel but as their spiritual overseer. It is the growth many wilderness leaders experience: from father to grandfather, from president to chairman of the board, from pastor to apostle.

The overseer is not only a man who discerns spirits; he is a man of spiritual discernment. As overseer, Moses was now leading not by might nor by power but by God's Spirit. It was a radical change from the man who started out by swinging his staff at the heads of those who opposed him. Now, though, he had a vision not just for a single battle but for the entire Kingdom.

The true overseer has the qualities attributed to the sons of Issachar in I Chronicles 12:32. It was said they "understood the times and knew what Israel should do." Moses had become that kind of man. While his young captain, Joshua, was in the valley with his sword, Moses was on the mountaintop with his rod stretched heavenward. He knew the battle was more than a military skirmish; it involved, at its heart, spiritual warfare.

Pastors may have insight, but the apostle has oversight. The apostle knows the direction the body should go and has a vision for the entire work. In the valley below, his "point man," Joshua, was leading the troops in victorious warfare. But General Moses had withdrawn, not for the sake of safety but in order to do the more important work—interceding and giving overall direction.

As the Israelites progressed in their own spiritual trek, drawing closer to the purposes of God, God did not always fight for them as He had done at the crossing of the sea. Now Israel was forced to fight also. Later, in the Promised Land, they would discover that although God promised them all the land where they set their feet, that land was invariably occupied by some enemy. No amount of "speaking a word of faith" would cause the enemy to flee. They had to physically force the enemy from the land. It was this combination of faith and works that brought them into final victory, both at Rephidim and in Canaan.

It was this lesson Moses wanted to teach his followers. Therefore, he turned the actual fighting over to a younger man, Hoshea, a prince of the tribe of Ephraim, whose name was changed to Joshua—"Jehovah is help."

It was an odd assortment of strategies: Joshua fighting with the sword while the overseer climbed the mountain with his two old companions—Aaron, his brother, and Hur, whom historian Josephus says was the husband of Moses' older sister, Miriam.

Even though Mt. Tahuneh, which Moses climbed, is only 750 feet above the valley floor, it is an arduous climb. I made that climb early one morning with a group of companions. The path was poorly marked, and very shortly our group was spread out over the precipitous face of the mountain like a flock of scattered mountain goats.

At one point I found myself in the middle of an ancient rockslide. I had no choice but to keep going, despite the cries from others to turn back. I realized I had to keep moving upward or be caught in a deluge of loose stones. Halfway up the steep ascent the slide began to move. Every place I put my feet, every place I put my hands, the rocks moved under me. It was an eerie feeling, and I was grateful for the shouts of encouragement from my friends, above and below, as I inched my way to safety and finally made it to the top. I thought of those three old men, climbing no doubt in the pre-dawn darkness to escape detection by the Amalekites who lived in the numerous caves, and I wondered how they had made it.

At the top, as the sun rose in the east over the blue range of the Sinai mountains, Moses took his place over the two armies now facing each other in the valley far below. As long as Moses held up his rod over the valley, the battle went in favor of the Israelites. When his hands dropped, the Amalekites surged ahead. Realizing what was at stake, Aaron and Hur moved a stone under Moses so he could sit down, then held his hands aloft until the sun set over Mt. Serabal in the southwest and the Amalekites were thoroughly defeated.

It is a thrilling story, and the lessons to be learned are of exceptional value to those of us on our own trek through the wilderness.

Primary is the absolute need for intercessory prayer when we come face-to-face with unconquerable enemies. While the battle in the valley is very real, the ultimate battle is always fought in the realm of the heavenlies. By holding up his hands, Moses was signifying he was in harmony with God— which is the essence of faith.

To the casual observer, it seemed Captain Joshua was winning a military battle. But a true analysis shows there was more taking place than the natural eye could see. The real battle was in the heavenlies as the angels of God battled the angels of darkness—a battle that is won only when the people of God join forces with the angels.

Over and over in the Scripture we see what happens when men, even two or three, come together in harmony with God. In the Upper Room 120 men and women were "all together in one place." As soon as they came into harmony with God's purpose, the Holy Spirit came as a mighty wind and filled the whole house where they were sitting. When a father came to Jesus on behalf of his dying daughter and linked his faith with the faith of Jesus, the daughter, who had actually died, came back to life. When Simon Peter withdrew to a bedroom and stood over the corpse of a dead child, singing the same song God was singing, the child breathed again.

It is this principle of faith that demands a father give "spiritual covering" to his family. When the father is not in his rightful place, the battle goes against them. But when the father occupies his place between God and the enemy, holding up his hands in intercession for his wife, his sons and daughters, his grandchildren—the battle in the valley below goes in favor of God's people.

Miracles always accompany faith. Faith allows God to flow unrestricted through a human instrument, as breath blows through a trumpet or flute, bringing God's music to earth. Rephidim, therefore, presents a beautiful picture of three old men in prayer, two holding up the hands of the third, turning the tide of battle for those below.

In earlier days Moses would never have thought of winning a battle except by using his staff to crack the head of an enemy soldier. But such victories, he now realized, often end in personal defeat, or at best are limited to skirmishes won but battles lost. In this case God said the victory won at Rephidim was complete. He told Moses to "write this on a scroll as something to be remembered and make sure that Joshua hears it, because I will completely erase the memory of the Amalekites from under heaven" (Exodus 17:14).

Later Moses did tell Joshua, "When the Lord your God

gives you rest from all the enemies around you in the land he is giving you to possess as an inheritance, you shall blot out the memory of Amalek from under heaven. Do not forget!" (Deuteronomy 25:19).

It was a needed admonition, for the enemies of God did not disappear at Rephidim. In fact, the "Amalekites" kept reappearing throughout Israeli history. Joshua had additional battles with them in Canaan. King Saul fought them. David had to fight them. Yet from the time of the battle at Rephidim there is no mention ever made of the name Amalek in non-biblical history. Even in biblical history they are referred to only by the name *shusa*. (In Hebrew, *shosehu* means "plundered.") But it is good to know that despite the constant reappearance in history of the enemies of God, they are a defeated people.

There is a final lesson, equally important, to be learned at Rephidim. The rod that Moses held up was the banner of God. It was the symbol of recognition that while man does the work, God gets the glory. After the battle was over and the Amalekites had been defeated, Moses took stones and built an altar on top of Mt. Tahuneh to perpetuate the event. He called the altar *Jehovahnissi*, "the Lord is my banner." He gave God the glory.

Whether it is modern political Israel or those who have been grafted into the branch and make up the Church, the people of God must continue to fight. But the victory is God's, and only as the people give God the glory is the victory guaranteed. The people of God have the rod of almighty power in Jesus Christ. As long as that rod is lifted toward heaven, whether it be over a field of snakes or over the warring hordes of the enemies of God, the victory is assured. When God is given the glory, the blessings secured by His covenant promise are always in force, even for those of us trekking through our own Rephidims on the way to the Promised Land.

XII

Leadership

"What is this you are doing for the people? Why do you sit alone as judge . . . ?"

(Exodus 18:14)

No burden is so heavy as the burden of leadership. I have been intrigued, therefore, to discover that one of the purposes of the wilderness is to teach us how to lead others. Indeed, Jesus said the heart of His ministry was to enlist men to become "fishers of men."

At the end of His earthly life, Jesus called His disciples around Him and said, "Therefore go and make disciples of all nations . . . teaching them to obey everything I have commanded you" (Matthew 28:19-20). Earlier, when these same men were together, Jesus told them: "As the Father has sent me, I am sending you." Then, breathing on them, He had said, "Receive the Holy Spirit" (John 20:21-22). His last words to Simon Peter came in the form of a commission to lead others: "Feed my lambs. . . . Take care of my sheep. . . . Feed my sheep" (John 21:15-17).

Like many great leaders, the character of Moses was a long time in formation. His great leadership was not due to some rare combination of personal gifts; rather, it was a gift from God developed and improved during his forty-year matriculation at Wilderness University.

Moses was a man like all of us, with flaws that veined the pure marble of his character, with a horrendous temper that

113

sometimes overshadowed his fabled meekness, and a stubborn will that was in constant conflict with his deep compassion and unselfishness. Like all of us, he was a man constantly wrestling with God—but always with the purpose of losing the match.

The character of the leader, however, is as dear to God as the work he is doing; and God spares no pains to complete the design to which He has set His hand. It is not surprising, therefore, that at the moment of Moses' greatest triumphs, God sent a man to speak a word of correction, and to change his way of ministry so radically that the entire structure of the Kingdom of God on earth was to be altered.

Few men can stand great or continued success. It is relatively easy to walk as a broken man, realizing that we are nothing and that God alone is worthy to be praised. But to receive the praise and accolades of others, to be looked upon as a "great man," as a "giant of the faith"—that is the path that causes the step of even the strongest to falter.

It is easier to be abased than to abound, to be empty than to be full, to rise from failure than to walk in success. Even though we continue to pray, and to utter the words "I give God the glory," how subtle the heart is turned until the time comes when we could well say with mad Nebuchadnezzar, "Is not this the great Babylon I have built as the royal residence, by my mighty power and for the glory of my majesty?" (Daniel 4:30).

But whenever this happens, when the heart of the leader is filled with pride and a feeling of self-accomplishment, there comes an end to his usefulness. God will not share His glory with anyone else. It is His solemn decree that no flesh shall glory in His presence.

This is why so many of God's servants, men who once led other men in remarkable ways, are laid aside. As long as they were weak, they were strong, but once they became strong in themselves, and began to listen to the praise of others, they became useless to God.

Tragic is the fall of any man; but especially tragic is the fall of a leader. Years spent in preparation, tears spent weeping at the feet of God, generations spent struggling through the wilderness—all lost and left behind when a man grows strong in himself and begins to imagine that what he has accomplished has been by his own strength, rather than by the grace of God. Such men may continue to preach, but their words no longer stir the dry bones with the breath of God. Such men are Samsons, going forth but not realizing the Lord has departed from them. They are like fishermen who think their loaded nets are due to their own expertise, instead of being the gift of the One who gathered the fish on that particular side of the boat.

Moses was in danger of such a fall. Everything had gone his way from the time he first accosted Pharaoh in his palace. For almost a year his life had been an uninterrupted stream of success. He had brought the world's proudest ruler to his knees. The elders of the ancient nation of Israel revered him. After all, God had chosen him to lead the world's greatest Exodus. His success was evidenced in the parted sea, the drowned army, the song of victory, the fall of the manna, the knowledge of the wilderness, the water from the rock, and then his latest victory over the Amalekites when all he did was climb the mountain and hold out his rod. No wonder the people flocked to him night and day as a man of superb wisdom and unlimited knowledge! All these things combined to place him in an unparalleled position of absolute authority and glory.

What an awesome position! What a frightening position! How easy it is, even in the wilderness, to imagine you have now learned all there is to learn and that the exaltation now coming your way is justified—indeed, deserved.

Therefore God, who was not ready for Moses to join the list of proud but useless ministers who sadden history's scroll, sent into his life a wise but humble man to puncture his balloon of ego. To whom could Moses submit? There was only one man who could be classified as his peer—or, even stronger, his superior. And God sent that man to Moses within days following the defeat of the Amalekites. He was Jethro, Moses' old mentor—and incidentally, his father-in-law—the only elder he had ever known.

The aged priest of Midian had been kept fully informed of the progress of his son-in-law, probably from the time Moses left Jethro, his wife, Zipporah, and his two sons to fulfill his promise to God to bring the Israelites back to Mt. Sinai. When the word came that Moses and his kinsmen had left Rephidim and were marching through the Naqb el Hawa—the "valley of the wind"—Jethro knew it was time to join him. Gathering his family about him, including Zipporah and the two sons who had been entrusted to his care, he traveled overland to meet Moses on the great plain that stretched forth from the base of Sinai—er Rakha.

After the customary salutations, the sharing of hospitality and the proper introductions, Moses and Jethro spent the night talking. Zipporah would have been scurrying around the tent, fixing food, making sure her husband was comfortable. Sitting crosslegged in Bedouin fashion, Moses told Jethro all God had done. Jethro listened intently and responded: "Praise be to the Lord . . . who rescued the people from the hand of the Egyptians. Now I know that the Lord is greater than all other gods, for he did this to those who had treated Israel arrogantly" (Exodus 18:10-11).

There followed first a time of worship, then a time of celebration. The family was once again united.

The next day the cloud that had been leading the Israelites through the deep wadis was stationary. Instead of moving, it hovered over the camp as though moored by an invisible cable. Moses took the opportunity to hold court, for he filled not only the role of senator and president, but chief justice as well. In fact, he also served as chief of police, county commissioner and head of the water and sewer division. He was also in charge of planning and zoning, the department of transportation, the department of agriculture, and was chief of veterinary medicine. But on this day an incident took place that was destined to change the course of governmental history, not only for the nation of Israel but for the entire world.

"The next day Moses took his seat to serve as judge for the people, and they stood around him from morning till evening" (Exodus 18:13).

It was Moses' time to shine in the presence of his old father-in-law. The last time Jethro had seen him, Moses was nothing more than an old shepherd heading out alone across the wilderness to rejoin his kinsmen in Egypt. Now he had returned as a great charismatic leader, revered, respected, leading an entire nation on a supernatural pilgrimage to a Promised Land. This was Moses' chance to invite his old teacher to come and see—to feel proud that his son-in-law had done so well in such a short period of time.

But Jethro's reaction was nothing short of startling. That night, as they sat again in their tent, Moses waited for Jethro's approval. Instead, the wizened old Bedouin, sitting crosslegged on the sand, looked across the fire and asked, "What is this you are doing for the people? . . . What you are doing is not good. You and these people who come to you will only wear yourselves out. The work is too heavy for you; you cannot handle it alone" (Exodus 18:14, 17-18).

Moses sat silently. How desperately he wanted Jethro's approval! Yet deep inside he sensed God was speaking. It was time to listen, not to grow defensive or to pout. He knew that the primary reason they were in the wilderness was to hear the voice of God. Why should he be exempt from teaching? If God was a God of change, as he had been teaching his followers, then it stood to reason there would be times when the leader himself would have to change.

Now was such a time. As he had for many years, Moses leaned forward to hear what his old teacher, the only father he had ever known, had to say.

"Listen now to me and I will give you some advice," Jethro began, "and may God be with you." Then he quickly outlined the five basic ingredients of spiritual leadership—things Moses needed to incorporate into his life if he were to minister effectively and not in his own strength.

1. You must be a priest—the people's representative before God.
2. You must be a teacher, teaching them the decrees and laws.
3. You must be an example, showing them the way to live and the duties they are to perform.
4. You must be an administrator, selecting capable men from all the people and appointing them as officials over thousands, hundreds, fifties and tens.
5. You must be a judge, having them bring the difficult cases to you but letting them decide the simple cases for themselves.

"If you do this and God so commands," Jethro finished, "you will be able to stand the strain, and all these people will go home satisfied" (cf. Exodus 18:19-26).

When God speaks through a man, the wise man of God will recognize the voice. Moses knew the wisdom coming from Jethro was the wisdom of God. He acted on the advice, and immediately established other men in the body to share in the leadership. Even though he would still be recognized as the head, others would share in the ministry—and God would get the glory.

It is never God's will for a man of God to burn himself out, even in service for God. God does not want us to overtax our machinery. It is man who drives slaves with a whip. God is never in a hurry. He causes clouds to pause, commands a Sabbath rest, and smiles when His servants slow down and relax. God realizes the weight of the burden of leadership. Therefore He has designed a plan that, if worked correctly, will provide not only rest for the leader but satisfaction for all the others called into service.

The wise leader knows it is much better to teach a man how to fish than to give him a fish, much better to enlist an army than to fight the enemy singlehandedly.

Many years later, the apostle Paul would take this same principle and apply it to the Church. He would point out there is a difference between the role of pastor and the role of apostle. He would tell the churches of the foolishness of expecting one man to be all things—preacher, spiritual overseer, evangelist, teacher and pastor. Each office is different, he said in Ephesians 4, and should be filled by different men. This way no single man is faced with the danger of taking the glory for himself, or of working himself into a premature grave and leaving the sheep shepherdless.

Long after Jethro had returned to Midian, Moses, who no longer seemed to need to be all things to all people, again divided the leadership responsibilities, backing off even further from the one-man rule.

Despite the fact that his pastors were functioning well in their jobs over the people, he still felt the burden of responsibility. He needed men, not only to perform the pastoral, administrative and judicial duties, but men who would stand with him as elders, to bear the burden of the entire body.

This time there was no Jethro to advise him. But this time none was needed. Moses had learned the lesson of shared responsibility—of multiple leadership. He realized the job was too big for him and he approached God, admitting the burden of spiritual responsibility was too heavy for one man to carry.

God told him to call out from the people seventy men who were already serving in some phase of leadership, older men who had proven themselves as leaders and officials. While these men had been active in the governmental activities of the nation, God was now going to set them apart as spiritual elders to share the burden with Moses. "I will take of the Spirit that is on you," He told Moses, "and put the Spirit on them. They will help you carry the burden of the people so that you will not have to carry it alone" (Numbers 11:17).

Still later, shortly before he died, Moses took a final step in sharing the leadership. He set apart Joshua as an apostle. "So the Lord said to Moses, 'Take Joshua son of Nun, a man in whom is the spirit, and lay your hand on him. . . . Give him some of your authority so the whole Israelite community will obey him'" (Numbers 27:18, 20).

The principle of leadership, as learned in the crucible of the wilderness, is the principle of change. God has no static government, nor does He allow men enough knowledge to form a static theology. The moment that happens, the moment we declare we know the full purpose of God in government or theology, that is the moment we discover the cloud has moved and we are no longer under it.

Jesus likened the Kingdom of God to new wine—always expanding, growing, changing. To pour such into a traditional, dried wineskin would be a disaster. Only as the wineskin remains flexible, He said, elastic and willing to change shape and size, can the Kingdom be contained.

Such is the danger of static leadership. Leaders are always expendable. The moment the leader feels he is necessary to God, he becomes useless to the people. Theology, too, must remain flexible, for men are always receiving new illumination on old truth which, if valid, must be applied to the lives of growing men.

Our concepts of God, therefore, must be always changing, ever growing. The true leader realizes he does not have a corner on truth but must lead with an open ear, not by some creed chiseled in stone but by listening to the ever-speaking voice of God. Books on theology, which are the manuals leaders must use, should always close with a semicolon, leaving space for new understanding as it comes in our wilderness journey.

The wilderness does not make leaders; it simply reveals them. Then, if they are wise, they will get on with the business of raising up other leaders—so the Kingdom may grow and God may get the glory.

XIII

Patience

Listen to the path; it is wiser than he who travels it.
—Bedouin proverb

In certain sections of the Sinai, the Bedouin gather honey from the date palms called *devash*. I've watched the women take the honey, complete with its comb, and place it in cloth sacks made of loosely woven material. This is suspended from the branch of a tree and allowed to drip slowly into containers placed below. It takes a long time, sometimes days, for the honey to ooze out of the comb and drip through the straining cloth into the urns.

Once I asked if I could hasten the process by squeezing the bag. The old woman shook her finger in my face, and from behind the black veil that covered her mouth told me that to squeeze the sack would streak the honey, making it less valuable.

There are certain wilderness lessons that cannot be learned in the rush of life, in the excitement of Egypt. These can be learned only in the slow process of trudging. Here, as we walk doggedly—sometimes blindly—through our personal wilderness, the dripping action takes place: for lessons are learned, not in rapid squeezing but in the perspective of time. In the wilderness the honeycomb of our reactions and incompleteness is left in the bag. Only what is pure oozes through to be collected in the urn.

My visits to St. Catherine's Monastery near the base of Mt.

Sinai always brought this to mind. The monastery is one of the most interesting places in the world. In the fourth century, Emperor Constantine and his mother, Empress Helena, embraced Christianity. In 327 A.D. the elderly Empress Helena undertook a pilgrimage to the Sinai. Near the base of Jebel Musa, she found a small community of hermits who pointed out what looked like a raspberry bush and told her it was the original burning bush. Helena ordered a small chapel to be built around the bush and dedicated it to the holy virgin. The chapel became the center of Christian activity in the high mountain region.

Two hundred years later, in 527 A.D., the small chapel was enlarged by Emperor Justinian into a formidable monastery, a fortress to protect the hermits from marauding bands of robbers. Sometime after that it was rededicated to St. Catherine, the virgin martyr of fourth-century Alexandria. It has been inhabited by monks and pilgrims for more than sixteen centuries, making it one of the oldest continuously occupied buildings in the world.

Nestled against the base of Jebel Safsafa, one of the towering red granite peaks of the Mt. Sinai cluster, the monastery is literally squeezed into a narrow wadi that immediately fans out to er Rakha, the wide plain where the Israelites camped while Moses was on the mountain. It has withstood the Islamic invasion of the seventh century, flashfloods, earthquakes and bands of marauding nomadic tribes for sixteen centuries. During this time it has housed a small group of Greek Orthodox monks whose sole task is to maintain the monastery.

Secluded in their utter remoteness, St. Catherine's monks have been known to let whole eras go by without notice. A visitor in 1946 was astonished to learn the monks had not heard of World War II and that some were unaware of World War I. They spend their time tending the ancient library, one of the oldest and richest in the world, constantly repairing the crumbling walls and walkways, and caring for the precious icons and the gold and silver ornaments that decorate the elegant chapel.

Since the Six-Day War in 1967, however, the outside world has forced itself on the abbey. An airport was built nearby. A paved road now runs through Wadi Feiran from the Gulf of Suez to the entrance of the monastery. Over the last years, before the Sinai was handed back to Egypt in 1982 (a decision that does not seem to affect the operation of the ancient monastery in the least), as many as 100,000 tourists a year descended on the black-frocked monks to disturb their tranquillity and gawk at the ancient artifacts and ornate chapel.

Although I much prefer the solitude of the desert to the bustling activity of the monastery and the somber attitudes of the monks, my visits to Jebel Musa have always led me back to St. Catherine's for brief visits. The water is the best in the Sinai; a visit to the charnal house where the bones of all the deceased monks lie exposed in bins awaiting the final resurrection is interesting; and occasionally one of the usually preoccupied fifteen monks will take time from his polishing and dusting to smile and pose for pictures.

After days of trekking through the desert with a small group of dusty pilgrims—cooking our own food in the open, camping out at night, climbing mountains and drawing water from the wells—we would finally arrive at the entrance to the ancient monastery.

Sometimes we would descend upon the fortress-looking building from the high mountain path, having spent the night on Mt. Sinai. Other times we would make our approach from the plain of er Rakha, either on foot or by camelback.

Each time, however, as I led my dusty, unshaved desert pilgrims into the monastery compound, I have been struck by the contrast we made to the groups of tourists who had flown in to the nearby airport or traveled overland by bus from Elat or Cairo.

These gawkers, dressed in their city clothes with necks hung with cameras, had only hours before left the comfort of their air-conditioned hotel rooms in a modern city. After a quick look at the monastery (some might stay long enough to climb Jebel Musa by the stone stairs, spending ten minutes on the summit taking more pictures), the tourists would hurry back to the airport or to their air-conditioned buses. Returning home, they would show their slides and proclaim themselves experts on the Sinai. After all, they had seen the mountain, talked to an old Bedouin (and perhaps, after paying him a dollar, mounted up on his camel for more pictures), and listened to the memorized lecture droned by some guide who knew better than to answer questions. The more venturesome might even have spent the night at one of the dormitory rooms at the monastery, but none would have dared enter the surrounding desert. They were all in too much of a hurry.

But a quick visit to the desert does no more make one an expert on the wilderness than a visit to a history class makes one an archaeologist.

Some things cannot be learned on the run. They must be learned slowly, as honey drips through the muslin delaine. They must be walked out through the experience of time. It is difficult to hear God on the run. Elijah discovered this truth many years after Moses learned the same thing. Not until the prophet got quiet and waited in the high oasis on the mountain was he able to hear.

So it is with all impatient men, for God is not seen by those in rapid transit. Isaiah heard only after he pulled aside from the throng of worshipers in the Temple and sat quietly in the presence of God. David heard Him on the hillside tending his lambs, alone with harp and flute. Jesus heard best when He withdrew from the mobs—even from His disciples—and took time to spend the night praying on some mountain, or kneeling alone in a garden. John the apostle, with nothing but the time of exile on his hands, heard Him as he waited patiently on the isle of Patmos.

The soft occasions, the quick squeezings of the bag, do not bring out the deepest of man. Only as he sinks his roots into the hard, rocky soil of the wilderness, only as he waits patiently for his bush to burn, only as he withdraws for his own forty days and forty nights of waiting, does he find his Source. The trouble, it seems, is that God is not in a hurry, and I am.

One of the great virtues learned in the wilderness is patience. In the desert you forget calendars. You leave your watch behind, for it is useless. You go to bed at sunset and rise at dawn. Meals are scheduled by body needs, not to satisfy clocks and appointments. In the desert, one learns to wait.

How programmed we are to produce! Goal-oriented, production-conscious, we have been trained to close each day with a question: How much did I produce today? Did I meet my quota? Everything is geared to what the production control people call "the bottom line"—which is preceded invariably by a dollar sign. It is a mentality developed by a materialistic society that places the prime emphasis on doing rather than being.

But in the wilderness, you learn patience. Here you have time—lots of it. There is time to grow still. Time to pull aside and look at a bush burn. Time to sit with friends and talk. Time to pray. Time to explore. Time to rest. Time to walk long distances without the anxiety of having to be back to meet a schedule. In the desert you rediscover the precious commodity of time. As faith has been boxed in by religious rites, so has time been relegated by our hurry-up society into a framework of calendars and clocks. Only in the wilderness do you discover how precious it is to have enough time to do what you want.

Perhaps it is best described in the desert term for time—the number *forty*. Over and over we find the term in our Bibles. Noah was in the ark forty days and forty nights. Moses was forty years old when he was exiled to the Sinai. He remained another forty years. He was on Mt. Sinai forty days and nights—two times. The twelve spies scouted out the land of Canaan for forty days. The children of Israel wandered for forty years. Elijah's journey into the wilderness lasted forty days. Jonah warned Ninevah they had forty days to repent. Jesus fasted in the wilderness forty days and nights, and when He appeared to His disciples following His resurrection, He was present forty days.

In many instances the term *forty* means a time of cleansing and preparation. But the term also appears in other contexts in the desert, especially in the Bedouin culture. There is a Moslem legend that 40,000 prophets have arisen out of Sinai since the beginning of time. Bedouin call the cold winter *el-arbiniyah*, the forty days. They also speak of a remedy for sickness called *el-arbain*, which is a mixture of forty plant species mixed with olive oil and butter. Forty days is the appointed time for mourning. The quail-hunting season lasts forty days. Flies pester the sheep and goats for forty days at the beginning of summer and forty days at the end of summer. If you are forty paces from the home of a man who gives you shelter, you are in a "safe zone" and cannot be attacked by a pursuing army.

What does the term *forty* really mean? Although the true meaning has been lost across the centuries, in nearly all cases it stems from the root meaning of *a long time.*

In the case of Moses' lifespan, and the time spent in the wilderness by the children of Israel, it is probably a literal term. In other instances, it is a general term that means simply "a long time." Even so, it must be remembered that forty is not a natural number, like the lunar or menstrual periods of thirty days. It is a supernatural number signifying preparation for importance. To that degree, it is not what happens during the "forty" days or years that is revelatory, but what takes place when the cycle is over—immediately afterwards. For Jesus, it was the beginning of His earthly ministry. The same holds true in the case of Moses—and most certainly with the corporate body of Israel. For all of them, the wilderness was not the real world; it was a place through which they passed—patiently—to be prepared for what lay ahead.

God may be found in the wilderness. But the entire scale of time and place in the wilderness is "utterly other," apart from time and space as we know it in our rapid-transit society.

In my times in the desert I have become aware of its ageless-ness and vastness. Each time I have entered the Sinai I have purposefully taken off my watch and left my appointment calendar behind. Here it makes no difference how old I am, what the date is, or whether it is 9:00 a.m. or noon. I have learned to get up with the dawn and crawl into my sleeping bag when the sun sets.

When I asked a Bedouin how long it would take to move his sheep to another pasture, he shrugged and replied, "Not long." When I asked what time tea would be served in his tent he said, "When the water boils." I still remember the smiles the Bedouin men gave me when, after eating a leisurely meal around their campfire at night, I asked when we as their guests should go to bed. "When you get sleepy," they laughed.

Each answer was given with a shrug—and a grin. In other words, Why be in such a hurry? You have plenty of time. Perhaps forty years.

So I have learned from these citizens of the desert, just as I have learned from the trees and plants. Desert trees do not bloom on command. The date palm, for instance, produces its fruit in its season. Then it waits patiently as the next crop is prepared. No amount of commands to "Hurry up!" will make it produce faster. It waits on God's time.

The psalmist said the blessed man is "like a tree planted by streams of water, which yields its fruit in season and whose leaf does not wither" (Psalm 1:3).

My times in the wilderness have taught me that God does not expect fruit every day—even the fruit of the Spirit. In fact, there have been times, after times of exasperation, when my only response to the situation is to mutter, "Damn!" That is different from grumbling. It is simply a commentary on how I felt.

God did not condemn Moses when he smashed the tablets of the Law in his thunderous reaction to finding the golden calf at the base of the mountain. He recognized there were limits to each man's ability to control his emotions. God had plenty of time, so He adjusted His schedule to allow another forty days and nights so Moses could cleanse his soul and once again hear God speak.

There are seasons when the man of God flourishes spiritually. Then there are times when the leaves of our life fall, the fruit disappears, and for all appearances our tree is lifeless. But each tree has a season, and in the proper season the fruit reappears.

I have walked through the agriculture experimentation stations in Israel where these industrious people have developed trees that produce fruit all year long. These trees have fruit and blossoms on their branches at the same time. But the fruit is never as tasty as that which comes from the tree that produces only once a year, then waits patiently for the next crop to mature.

The psalmist equates the "blessed man" with a tree "planted by streams of water." It is a strange simile when you consider the wilderness, for there are no such rivers in the desert. The best you can find is a dry riverbed, a wadi, which is filled with water only on occasion.

The difference is profound. Any tree can produce when

planted on the shores of a sparkling river. But in the wilderness, where there are no rivers, the fruit trees need to find nourishment in another way. The beautiful date palm, for instance, which produces the most delicious of all desert fruit, finds water by sending its roots into the underground reservoirs. It does not depend on showers of blessings to keep it producing, but draws its strength from the hidden nourishment found deep in the soil of the wilderness.

This is the lesson of the desert. When your branches are barren, when all your buds have dried up, when your leaves droop in discouragement—remember your roots. Remember that just beneath the sand there are underground reservoirs where the water is pure. Relax. Take your time. And know that in your season, you shall bear fruit again.

XIV

Intercession

"But now, please forgive their sin—but if not, then blot me out of the book you have written."

(Exodus 32:32)

The ascent to Mt. Sinai is one of the most torturous, yet one of the most exhilarating experiences known to humankind.

Leaving Rephidim, I have often had to decide which of the two approaches to the Mountain of God I would take. The first is called "The Pilgrim's Path" of Naqb el Hawa—the valley of the wind. It is the traditional footpath that ends at the plain of er Rakha—the place of rest. The path is too narrow and precipitous for the vast hordes of Israelites to have traveled. Although I love to walk the seven miles or so from the tomb of Sheikh Awad to the plain of er Rakha, I suspect the children of Israel must have come east from Rephidim through Wadi esh Sheikh, then turned south past what is now the tomb of Sheikh Nabi Salh to approach the mountain.

Wadi esh Sheikh is the longest, widest and most continuous of the wadis in southern Sinai. On either side the Israelites saw the precipitous mountains rearing their inaccessible ramparts of red sandstone and variegated granite. Ibex, the long-horned mountain goat with antlers curling backwards in a great circle, peered down on them from lofty positions. Gazelle skipped across the open valley before them, darting quickly into the shadows. From the caves the huge spotted leopards growled and slunk backwards into the darkness. The wadis opening on the sides appeared as majestic corridors of a vast temple, with the pillar of cloud ushering them from the narthex of Rephidim through the sanctuary of Wadi esh Sheikh to the high altar of Mt. Sinai.

From either approach you suddenly enter, without warning, the perfectly level plain of er Rakha. Two miles long and a half-mile wide, it is dotted with broom bushes and small rocks. The mountains that gather around this plain have sloping sides and form a natural amphitheatre. Only on the southern end does the terrain change. There, jutting out of the sand of the desert and towering up into the azure blue sky, is the massive stone Mountain of God. Deeply cleft with fissures, and torn as though it has struggled to push its way up from the desert floor, it is a mountain touched by the hand of God and burned with fire.

Here, in this awesome wilderness sanctuary, the pilgrims were to receive new revelation concerning the character of God. All they knew of Him up until this time was He was a God of no name and no image who talked with Moses. Now they were to discover new and startling aspects of His nature.

When God established His covenant with Abraham, He revealed Himself as *El Shaddai*, a term meaning simply "God Almighty." At the burning bush, He told Moses He was not only El Shaddai, the God of Abraham, Isaac and Jacob; He went ahead to say He was *ehyeh asher ehyeh*—"I am that I am." At this point, God declared He was more than the essence of being, which is the root of the verb *I am*. He said He was the cause of being—underived existence coupled with an independent and uncontrolled will.

On Mt. Tahuneh Moses went a step further and called Him Jehovah-nissi—"The Lord is my banner." On Mt. Sinai, however, God came to Moses and called Himself by a far more personal name. The true pronunciation has long since been lost, but it is represented by the four Hebrew letters *YHWH*. It was lost because the Jews—except for the high priest—have scrupulously avoided ever mentioning it aloud. Instead, when they used it they always substituted another Hebrew word—Adonai. (According to Jewish tradition, *YHWH* was pronounced but once a year by the high priest on the Day of Atonement when he entered the Holy of Holies.)

Thus the name of God was not only kept at arm's length; it

was never to be looked upon, much less spoken, so sacred was it. When the Scriptures were written, there was need to call God *something*, so the writers added vowel points (which had not been used in the original writing since the old alphabet was only consonants) and *YHWH* became *Yahweh*. This was translated out in the later renderings as Jehovah—the self-existent God. This name, Yahweh or Jehovah, has its roots in *ehyeh*—underived existence.

During the march from Egypt to Mt. Sinai, God spoke basically to Moses. Only on rare occasions, such as at the springs of Marah, did the people hear His voice. The rest of the time He was reflected in the pillar of cloud by day and the column of fire at night—the God of no name and no image.

The revelation of the law on Mt. Sinai had a great impact, since now the God of history, the God of underived existence, made Himself known. Bit by bit, in a process known as progressive revelation, God revealed Himself—first to Moses and then to the people.

In the biblical account of the meetings between God and Moses on Mt. Sinai, a marvelous progression of familiarity begins to take place. It begins with the formal statement in Exodus 19:3: "Then Moses went up to God, and the Lord called to him from the mountain. . . ."

Following this, Moses descended to the plain to report to the people. Twice more he ascended the mountain, each time coming back to warn the people of God's holiness.

On the third day, the mountain began to rumble. It was covered with a dark cloud with lightning flashes and the pealing sound of angelic trumpet blasts. With the people standing in awe around the base of the mountain, having consecrated themselves and having been warned not to touch the sides of the mountain until they heard the long blast from the shofar—the ram's horn—they waited in awed silence as Moses once again ascended the mountain and disappeared into the dark cloud.

But it was not yet time to receive the commandments. Instead God, in a revelation of love and caution, told Moses to descend once again and make sure the people understood the nature of His holiness—how they would be destroyed if they disobeyed.

It is not clear whether Moses climbed to the peak of the

mountain, which extends almost 4,500 feet above the plain. But for the 80-year-old man it was a powerful effort. Once more the weary Moses descended, warned the people, then for the fourth time ascended again, this time taking his brother Aaron with him.

While Aaron listened in stunned silence, God spoke the words of the Ten Commandments and certain other ordinances. God again told Moses of the Promised Land and His desire for the people to move with dispatch and possess it. If they would obey Him, He said, they would not be sick, nor would the pregnant women miscarry their babies despite the hardships of the journey. He would send hornets to drive out the enemy as the Israelites approached the Promised Land. (This promise came true when the Israelites many years later marched against the Jebusites in Transjordan. At that time swarms of hornets routed the enemy, making their defeat certain.) It was a wonderful revelation of a loving and gracious God who promised to care for and protect His people as long as they obeyed Him.

Moses returned to the people and told them all God had said. Relieved and excited, they responded with one voice: "Everything the Lord has said we will do" (Exodus 24:3).

Moses then took the rest of the day to write down all the Lord had spoken. Early the next morning he built an altar at the foot of the mountain and prepared the people to receive the covenants of God. Then, for the fifth time, he climbed back up the mountain. Once again Aaron, the elders, and a few others went with him. Partway up, they came to a small oasis—a natural amphitheatre—called a *farsh*. They paused and suddenly God appeared. The entire peak of the mountain, which can be seen clearly from the farsh, became as sapphire, so powerful was His presence and so great His glory.

God called to Moses out of His glory, telling him to climb even higher. From the elders he chose only Joshua to accompany him, sending Aaron and Hur back down to watch over the people who waited below. Leaving Joshua partway up the trail to the summit, he climbed on to the peak alone. There he received not only the Ten Commandments, written on tablets of stone by the finger of God, but specific instructions on the erection of the tabernacle.

Descending the mountain with Joshua, he discovered the people had forgotten all their vows to be faithful. They had taken their golden rings and bracelets, melted them down and molded a golden calf—similar to the Egyptian Apis-bull that had been worshiped by Pharaoh.

To exalt the bull and give it divine status was a relapse into the Egyptian religion. Moses was outraged by the backsliding of his people who just days before had vowed, "Everything the Lord has said we will do." Raising the stone tablets over his head, he smashed them to the ground. It was a symbol that the covenant was declared null and void, for until the people actually received the tablets, the covenant was not in force. He blamed Aaron for the calf, who offered one of the most feeble excuses recorded in the Bible. "I don't know what happened," Aaron lamented. "All we did was throw the gold into the fire and out came this calf."

Realizing that Aaron was not capable of leading, that he had let the people run wild and could not control them, Moses called the people together and said, "Whoever is for the Lord, come to me."

His own tribe, the Levites, gathered around him. Moses then gave them a terrible command to take swords and kill all those who had led the rebellion. Even though the scene sounds grisly, God meant what He said when He warned the people that He was a holy God, that His commands were not to be taken lightly. That day more than 3,000 Israelites were slaughtered—and the revolution was put quickly to a finish.

The following day, his anger abated, Moses said to the people: "You have committed a great sin. But now I will go up to the Lord; perhaps I can make atonement for your sin" (Exodus 32:30).

What happened on the mountain that last trip has no comparison in history save what happened many years later at Calvary. Confessing the sin of his people, Moses took the place of the lonely advocate between God and the people. He was convinced of God's justice and did not see how God could go back on His solemn threat to destroy the nation. Yet if that judgment were to be averted, it must be in consequence of an atonement. The only thing he could offer was himself. Yet, he wondered, was even that enough?

Someplace along the line, during his conversations with

God, he had come to understand God was not only a God of justice; He was a God of mercy. And even though words like *lovingkindness* and *our Father* were yet to be defined, Moses had learned through his wilderness wanderings that only by suffering could one redeem another. It was the law of substitution. In deep pathos, therefore, the prince and leader of the nation fell on his face before God and proposed that he, the chosen servant, should be weighed in the scale against the people, and that God should accept his blood as a ransom for their life.

"Oh, what a great sin these people have committed! They have made themselves gods of gold. But now, please forgive their sin—" His words faltered. He could speak no more, as this supreme gesture on his part was choked by a paroxysm of grief, a sob of irrepressible emotion.

Finally, the words came forth: " . . . But if not, then blot me out of the book you have written" (Exodus 32:31-32).

Years later Jesus would remind His followers that this concept of self-sacrifice reflects the very heart of God's purpose for the world. "Greater love has no one than this, that one lay down his life for his friends" (John 15:13).

Moses had learned the ultimate lesson of the wilderness— that the love of God will cause us to give ourselves fully and completely for others.

Of course, the offer was rejected. No one but Messiah can atone for the sins of others. Yet because of the offer, God spared the people. It would be up to the Son of God to pay the price of "sins committed beforehand [which had gone] unpunished" (Romans 3:25).

Once more Moses remained on the mountain forty days. It was his last visit to Mt. Sinai. Returning to the people the final time, he carried with him two more tablets of stone. Where the first ones had been written by the finger of God, these had been laboriously chipped out by Moses' own hand. The covenant was complete. The people had been saved. Now it was time to head north toward Kadesh-Barnea, and the final siege of Canaan under the banner of God.

XV

Living Commandments

"If you make an altar of stones for me, do not build it with dressed stones, for you will defile it if you use a tool on it."
(Exodus 20:25)

It seems strange that God would give commandments knowing the people could not keep them.

The first high priest, Aaron, broke the second commandment even before the tablets of stone were handed over to the people. Moses broke the third when he misused the name of God by striking the rock after the Lord told him to speak to it only. Every one of the Ten Commandments was broken by the people before they got away from Mt. Sinai—and they have continued to be broken to this day.

If the Ten Commandments were impossible to keep, then why were they given? They were given to reveal the nature of God. For God is far more interested in a people who want to establish a relationship with Him than in a people who keep all the rules but never learn to abide in His presence.

In the wilderness one quickly realizes there are certain rules that, if flaunted, bring death. To drink poisoned water means death. To put your hand into the hole of a carpet viper or cobra means death. To wade in the shallow water off the coast of Aqaba and step on a stone fish means death. To eat the flesh of pork, which is often filled with trichinae, could mean death.

Even more important than the rules, however, is the relationship. The man who does no more than keep the rules dies.

But the man who sees the law, any law, as a means to know God, comes into a relationship that brings him into life.

Thus, even though the poisonous carpet vipers and black mambas that bit the Israelites in the wilderness meant death, when they looked upward to God (symbolized by the brazen serpent raised on a staff) they found life.

No sooner had God given His Ten Commandments to Moses than He began sharing some specific ordinances—rules for behavior dealing with the interpretation of the Commandments. One of the first of these had to do with the construction of altars.

"If you make an altar of stones for me," God told Moses, "do not build it with dressed [cut or hewn] stones, for you will defile it if you use a tool on it" (Exodus 20:25).

For ten generations the Israelites had been chiseling stones—stones to be used in the altars, idols and tombs of Egypt. The pyramids, those sacred tombs of the Egyptian pharaohs, were made of hewn stone. The Hebrew slaves had spent their last years in Egypt making bricks, shaped to fit into place in man's altars to false gods.

Now God was revealing a new concept. Jehovah, unlike all the Egyptian gods, did not need shaped stones. He did not need man's efforts for acceptable worship. He preferred the natural things—altars made of naturally shaped stones that had never been touched by hammer or chisel.

There is a sameness about bricks which is common to people in bondage and slavery. Bricks and hewn stones are made to conform. There is never any variation allowed. All are made to fit exactly into a designated place, with little or no irregularity or originality allowed or needed.

Slavery always produces bricks. Whether it is in the tone of the voice, the cut of the hair or clothes, the vocabulary one uses—you can always tell a person who is in bondage because he sounds and looks just like everyone else. Uniqueness is quenched. Individuality is not allowed. Genuine creativity is limited to products that look like those produced yesterday, and like those produced by everyone else.

Earlier Moses complained to God that instead of a disciplined army, he was being forced to lead a nation of uncut stones. Not a single one of them seemed to "fit." On a number of occasions Moses was tempted to chip them to shape, to make them conform to the image he felt they should take. Each time God said, "Hands off! I will do it. It is My job to conform each man to the shape I want him to take. I am the Master Builder who fits each stone into his place."

Each group of men I have taken with me into the Sinai has been composed of such "uncut stones"—strongly individualistic men who in most cases had never met each other until we set out for the wilderness. Despite every well-intentioned promise to "walk peaceably" with each other during the two-week trek through the wilderness, by the fourth or fifth day the veneers would begin to wear off. On several occasions the situations became downright explosive.

Stuck for 1,400 miles on a six-wheel-drive truck bouncing along through the wadis between mountains on trails that no ordinary vehicle could traverse, miles from any semblance of civilization, we discovered something quickly: we had to get along with the group despite our individuality. To leave the group would mean death in the desert. To expel one of the men from the group, no matter how badly he was behaving, would mean sending him to his death.

I remember one trip on which a conflict began to develop between two of the strongest-willed men—one a physician who is a marathon runner, and the other a jut-jawed, highly opinionated minister.

Tension had been building because the minister was free with his opinions about some of the men who were not measuring up spiritually. Most of the men had backed away from this "uncut stone," concluding the desert was no place to confront a prophet.

The physician, although easygoing in attitude, was intensely disciplined. Up each morning before the rest of us were out of our sleeping bags, he would run eight to ten miles across the desert sand before the sun got too hot. Then came the day when he told our guide he would run on ahead of the truck while the rest of us swam in an oasis near what was then the Egyptian border.

By the time the truck finally caught up with him ten miles later, several of the men in the group were worried. He had not taken a canteen and was running without the protection of a shirt—which is sheer folly in the desert. When we finally caught up with him, running happily along the Gulf of Suez in Egyptian territory, even I was relieved.

When the doctor climbed into the truck, however, the minister exploded in a fury of condemnation. What right did he have, the minister wanted to know, to leave the group in such a dangerous locale? In addition, the minister thought running was an unhealthy obsession, and he proceeded to tell him so in pointed terms.

The air was tense. I sensed a confrontation brewing between these two rough stones—a confrontation that could be painful to all of us since we were all thrust together in this venture.

That night around the campfire, several of the men told the minister he had lacked tact in his remarks on the truck. That led to a rehash of what had happened. The doctor apologized for scaring everyone, but said his running had merely become part of his lifestyle; it wasn't an obsession.

Unfortunately, this didn't satisfy the minister who, true to his prophetic calling, wanted to point out a few other faults he had noticed. The group took this for a few minutes and finally the doctor, in a straightforward manner, looked across the campfire at the minister.

"I am not nearly as concerned for you as I am for your wife. She must have to go through hell living with you."

It was like pouring gunpowder on a smoldering fire. Not since Moses cursed the followers of Korah had the desert heard such a reaction as we experienced that night around the campfire.

Finally one of the men told the minister that he had no right to dish out criticism unless he could also take it. He pointed out that the minister had just reacted in a way he had said was wrong for others.

The confrontation between the two was a watershed for our trip. The minister was more subdued during the rest of the time in the desert. The doctor was more careful to stay with the group. And the fact that the group had participated in that open confrontation brought everyone closer. Instead of being just a group of American men on a trip to the Sinai, we became a body of believers—uncut stones fitted together by the hand of God to form an altar pleasing to Him.

It was this same wilderness lesson Moses finally learned, and eventually taught to his followers. God does not want us all to look alike, behave alike, even believe alike. But He does want us to get along together without trying to fashion ourselves in the image of others, or trying to force others into our own image.

Shortly after the people left Mt. Sinai on their way north to Kadesh-Barnea, Moses called seventy men out of the tribes and ordained them as spiritual elders over the entire nation. The ordination service was held in the outer court of the tabernacle, but two men for some unknown reason missed the service. Eldad and Medad remained in the camping area. When the Spirit of God fell on the other 68 men, however, and they began to prophesy, the same phenomenon happened to Eldad and Medad on the other side of the campground.

A young man came running to Moses: "Eldad and Medad are prophesying in the camp."

Immediately Joshua, a bit jealous that the rules were being bent, objected. And Moses replied sternly, "Are you jealous for my sake? I wish that all the Lord's people were prophets and that the Lord would put His Spirit on them!" (Numbers 11:26-29).

Eldad and Medad were uncut stones, and Moses knew better than to try to hew them into his (or Joshua's) image. If God wanted to use them even though they did not fit the mold, that was God's business, not his.

It is this individualistic nature that has kept God's word alive and burning in the hearts of men across the centuries. Men such as Theodor Herzl, Eliezer Ben Yehuda and David Ben Gurion kept the dream of the Jewish nation alive in the hearts of men, even though they were viewed by most around them as uncut stones. Others, often cast as misfits in society—men such as John Hus, Martin Luther, John Wesley, and a host of contemporary uncut stones—have been instrumental in spreading the gospel of the Kingdom, despite their strange ways and sometimes odd behavior. Surely it is this concept the Lord wants kept alive in all of us!

I have in the front of my Bible a note I scribbled to myself a number of years ago that reminds me of God's purpose in my own life. It says simply, "Jamie, don't let the world—or the institutional church—fashion you into its mold."

The Lord reveals to those who walk through tough times that true worship of Him is never relegated to the places of hewn stone. Much later Jesus mentioned this same principle when He spoke to a Samaritan woman drawing water from Jacob's well near the little town of Sychar. "Our fathers worshiped on this mountain," she said, pointing to the top of nearby Mt. Gerazim, "but you Jews claim that the place where we must worship is in Jerusalem."

Jesus answered prophetically when He said, "A time is coming and has now come when the true worshipers will worship the Father in spirit and truth, for they are the kind of worshipers the Father seeks. God is spirit, and his worshipers must worship in spirit and in truth" (John 4:19-24).

The wilderness teaches us that God is not so interested in rules as He is in relationships. It is true that God puts conditions on His beloved and limitations on His children. But as we walk with Him through the wilderness, we gradually get our eyes off His rules and onto His face.

The Israelites had been in slavery for ten generations. Now they were free, but in their newfound freedom they became freewheeling. They said, "We can do anything we want." God therefore put severe restrictions on them—not to destroy their creativity, but to channel it into productive areas. Very patiently, very gently, He brought them to Himself. He showed them that in order to have complete freedom they had to be a people under authority, for true happiness comes only when we are in submission to God, and to one another.

Later in God's history, we find the Law was not meant to be an end, but a means to a greater end. The Ten Commandments, although they are not to be flaunted, were given primarily to reveal the character and nature of God. If all we do is try to keep the rules, we will ever be in slavery. But if we use the rules to move in closer to God, then we discover the laws are not chains that hold us down but guideposts that describe the character of a God who wants to reveal Himself to us.

The problem is not whether we work on the Sabbath, but

rather, What kind of God is He? What is He like? Why does He tell us to rest?

God is like our father, so we honor our father and mother.

God gives us life, so we do not murder.

God owns all things, so we do not steal.

God hallows marriage, so we do not commit adultery.

That is the purpose of the commandments—to reveal God. It is not doing what He says that brings life; it is abiding in His presence that keeps us alive.

God told Moses, therefore, "Build Me altars of unshaped stones. Each worshiper is precious to Me, regardless of shape or color. I love them, sharp edges and all, and can use them to build a Kingdom, if you let Me do the fitting."

"As you come to him," Peter said centuries later, "the living Stone—rejected by men but chosen by God and precious to him—you also, like living stones, are being built into a spiritual house to be a holy priesthood, offering spiritual sacrifices acceptable to God through Jesus Christ" (I Peter 2:4-5).

"The power of sin is the law," the apostle Paul said, referring to man's tendency to force everything into a mold. "But thanks be to God! He gives us the victory through our Lord Jesus Christ" (I Corinthians 15:56-57).

XVI

Silence

*"When my glory passes by, I will put you in a cleft in the rock
and cover you with my hand."*

(Exodus 33:22)

The most awesome aspect of the desert, perhaps the most terrifying aspect, is its total silence.

No place on earth is as silent as the Sinai. To those of us surrounded by noise, who have grown accustomed to the "madding crowd," the silence of the desert quickly becomes a fearsome thing.

For most people, silence creates a nervousness, an anxiety that forces us to seek noise; and if we do not find it, to create it. To some, silence becomes a gaping abyss that swallows us up, forcing us to turn inward to the even more awesome wilderness of self-understanding and self-revelation. To others, silence is the playground of our demons, which we keep fenced in only by our much talking and much activity. To grow silent opens the gates. Thus we fear the silence and go to great lengths to escape it.

We live in a society tormented by words, both spoken and written. The resulting inward noise remains, echoing through the chambers of our minds long after the shouting and whispering have ceased. Words form the floors, walls and ceilings of our thoughts. Indeed, we cannot think without them. They come at us from electronic boxes, from signboards, from the printed page, from jangling telephones, from pulpits, bumper stickers and magazines. They form the houses of our existence.

One writer relates that driving through a large city he suddenly had the strange sensation of driving through a huge dictionary. Everywhere he looked there were words saying, "Use me, take me, buy me, drink me, eat me, smell me, touch me, kiss me, sleep with me." These words have nested like parasites in every nook and cranny of our existence. They suck the life from us while deceiving us into believing we cannot live without them. To think conceptually, without letting our minds form the ideas into paragraphs and sentences, is an art lost to the Western world.

To soothe these words, we accompany them with music. If we are not singing them, we use music to back them up, to make them more palatable to our jangled spirits. Prayers in church are accompanied by background music. Soap is sold with a tune. Armies march to the sound of fife and drum. Drama on television and the screen always seems incomplete without the ever-present background of strings, brass and woodwinds. The dentist pulls our teeth to Muzak. We buy our clothing to the soft sound of violins and harps. We take our seats on the airlines to the accompaniment of melodies piped in through the "sound system." We have wedding music, funeral dirges, lullabies and music for every season. It is a marvelous world of harmonic sound—all composed to fill the silence we so fear.

Even without our words and music, there is still noise. The clanking of machinery, the whir of gadgets, the roar of the wind, the crashing of the surf, the buzz of insects day and night. There are street noises, factory noises, swamp and forest noises. There is the cawing of crows and the mooing of cows, the swish of wind through the grass, the crackling of the fire, the splashing of rain, the creaking of the floor, the sighs of lovers and the patter of tiny feet. All the world is full of sound.

But the desert is silent. Here there are no insects, no chirping katydids, no croaking frogs. Even the wind is silent as it blows noiselessly across the barren sand. The silence is so loud it is frightening. Yet it is here, in the silence, that God speaks loudest.

Elijah experienced this during his stay on Mt. Sinai. Having fled for his life, he arrived exhausted and despondent. Collapsing near a spring in a high mountain oasis halfway up the steep ascent to the summit, the troubled prophet had to wait until the wind, earthquake and fire of his inner man was quieted before he was able to hear the still, small voice of God.

Vivid in my memory is a chilly November night spent at the base of Mt. Sinai. Although I had spent many nights in the desert, this was my first time to sleep at the base of the Mountain of God at the 4,000-foot level. That night, although the temperature dropped below freezing, I lay on my back in my sleeping bag, my hands folded beneath my head to cushion it from the pebbly rocks, and stared upward at the unbelievable canopy of stars overhead. The outline of Jebel Musa—Mt. Moses—was an awesome granite shadow against the glistening black of the sky with its billions of flashing pinpoints of yellow and green. It was cold—and silent. I remembered something an old monk had written, hundreds of years before, of his first experience in the Sinai: "It is the silence that speaks the loudest."

That night, looking up into the magnificent display of God's creation in the heavens, a cosmorama that yet defies description, I, too, experienced the silence of Moses and Elijah—an outer silence that only accented the noise within. It started when I heard, for the first time in my life, my own heart pumping blood through my veins. Turning my head, I could hear the bones of my neck rasping together. But it was the deeper noise that caused the ultimate distraction. The moans of things left behind. The clatter of anxiety for things to come. The ping of guilt. The rumble of fears. The sigh of memories. The tearing sound of homesickness. That night, at the base of the holy mountain, I understood why God had to keep Moses alone for forty days and nights before Moses could hear Him speak. For God speaks in silence, and silence is hard to come by.

Earlier, when Moses made his descent from the mountain, his arrival in the camp of the Israelites was heralded by discordant sound. The people had in his absence created a golden calf to fill the void. The noise was the sound of their idol worship.

When Moses returned to the Mountain of God, after having

destroyed the golden calf and smashed the covenant stones, he had to wait another forty days and nights before he could once again hear God. His spirit, too, had been polluted by the clashing of ideas, his silence broken by the sounds of sin. To enter into that place of holiness where God abides—the place of absolute silence—once again he had to allow his spirit to be purged of sound. For the inner man is constantly tormented by noise.

"Be still before the Lord," Zechariah warned all mankind, ". . . because he has roused himself from his holy dwelling" (Zechariah 2:13).

"Be silent before the Sovereign Lord," echoed Zephaniah (Zephaniah 1:7).

It is silence that gives meaning to the Word of God. Someone has said the Bible is the Word of God rather than the words of God. This is so, for in grasping the Word we begin to hear His words, spoken in the silence of our own hearts.

The desert fathers, those early hermits who fled to the Sinai in the third and fourth centuries to seek personal salvation, were in reality trying to escape from the noise of the world. Although they eventually died away—for their purpose of living was all inward with little understanding of the need to share—they did leave one valid contribution. They taught us the value of silence. Somehow they believed they could best find God in silence—and knew of no place more silent than the Sinai.

There is a delightful story about one of those early hermit leaders who had moved to the desert in the third century. His name was Abbot Macarius. When he had finished blessing his small group of desert dwellers, he said to them, "Brethren, flee." One of the men, puzzled, asked, "How can we fly further than this, seeing we are here in the desert?" Macarius looked at him. Placing his finger on his mouth, he said, "Flee from this." It was his personal vow of silence. He then turned, entered his small cell carved from the rock and shut the door. It was his way of saying what the prophet had said long before him: "The Lord is in his holy temple; let all the earth be silent before him" (Habakkuk 2:20).

"I have often repented of having spoken," Abbot Arsenius said, "but never of having remained silent."

It was this same concept that motivated Benedict, the father of monastic life. He put great emphasis on silence as a way of life, believing that only when the human heart was stilled could the still, small voice be heard. Benedict went on to warn his followers against not only evil talk, but against all talk. Speaking when one should remain silent could quickly lead one away from God and into the path of calling attention to self. Like the desert fathers, he believed that "every conversation tended to interest them in this world, to make them less of strangers and more of citizens."

St. John of the Cross used to refer to the times when his "house was all stilled." During this process, the emotional, psychological, physical, even spiritual dwellers all sat down and grew quiet. All distractions ceased and God finally spoke.

The Way of Silence is foreign to those of us who work with words, whose lives are spent communicating on a horizontal level. Yet Moses discovered that when he was silent vertically, he was then able to speak before the people. It's sad, but what many speakers hope to be their finest hour—ministering to the multitudes—is often the time of greatest emptiness for speaker as well as listener. Yet when we wait silently before God, we often come away refreshed, the fire of our inner man refueled, able to say in few words what would have ordinarily taken hours.

One of these early hermits, Abbot Agatho, carried a stone in his mouth for three years until he learned to be silent. A modern mystic, Henri Nouwen, writes: "As soon as we begin to take hold of each other by our words, and use words to defend ourselves or offend others, the world no longer speaks of silence. But when the word calls for the healing and restoring stillness of its own silence, few words are needed and much can be said without much being spoken."

Silence is often equated—or at least linked in our minds—with darkness. Yet men of wisdom have learned, as Moses did on Mt. Sinai, that God dwells in the darkness. When God called Moses to the summit of the mountain to receive the Law, the entire mountain was covered with a thick cloud. As Moses ascended, he disappeared from sight to the people watching from below. The cloud grew darker until he was in total darkness. Yet here he found God. This was later confirmed by the shepherd king, David, who discovered that even the darkness is not dark to God. Indeed, "the night will shine like the day, for darkness is as light to you" (Psalm 139:12).

Perhaps this cannot be fully understood unless you, too, have walked in the darkness of the wilderness. Surely this is one of the great purposes of our wilderness experience, to teach us the value of total silence—to train us to listen to the still, small voice of God and to feel His presence in the darkness. Here in the wilderness, we discover that even the valley of the shadow of death holds no fear, "for thou art with me."

One afternoon I inquired of that lovable old Dutch saint Corrie ten Boom about the silence and the darkness of God. Years before, when she was 50 years of age, she had been forced into a Nazi concentration camp. There her old father and dear sister died horrible deaths. Yet out of that wilderness she learned the truth of Psalm 91:1: "He that dwelleth in the secret place of the most High shall abide under the shadow of the Almighty" (KJV).

She was 80 when I talked to her. "Even though we are to walk in the light with our brothers and sisters," she told me, "there comes a time, as you draw close to God, that you are consumed with darkness. This is true when you are abiding in the shadow. The closer you get to God, the less you understand Him. In the darkness of His presence, under the shadow of the Almighty, we learn to believe."

It is the difference between sight and faith. Sight—knowledge—is the breeding ground for noise and words. Faith, however, calls for silence. There we do not speak. This is the reason many men of faith are men of few words. What they have experienced defies description. It must be experienced, lived, not communicated.

Faith, we are often told, is not taught; it is caught.

In the thirty-third chapter of Exodus, there is a marvelous parenthetical story that describes the lesson Moses learned on Mt. Sinai. After descending from the mountain of darkness, and before the tabernacle became the official "tent of meeting" where man and God had their conversations, Moses had his own little place of silence. It was a small tent that he pitched outside the camp, some distance away from the mob of Israelites with all their noise. It was his version of what Jesus was later to describe as a "prayer closet." To Moses, it was his own "tent of meeting." When Moses would go outside the camp and enter this little tent, the pillar of cloud would come down and stay at the entrance. There, in total silence, the Lord spoke to Moses. It was their way of recreating the experience on Mt. Sinai.

"Whenever the people saw the pillar of cloud standing at the entrance to the tent, they all stood and worshiped, each at the entrance to his [own] tent." Then, when all the camp grew silent, "the Lord would speak to Moses face to face, as a man speaks with his friend" (Exodus 33:7-11).

It was during one of these long, solitary sessions that God told Moses, "My Presence will go with you, and I will give you rest" (Exodus 33:14).

Moses could contain himself no longer. Racing from the tent, he clambered up the side of the huge mountain that towered over the Israelites as they camped on the er Rakha plain at the base of Mt. Sinai. Panting more from exhilaration than exhaustion, he finally reached the top. There, standing far above all earthly sound where even the wind blowing in mighty gusts was freezingly silent, Moses lifted his voice and cried out to God: "Now show me your glory!"

The biblical description of this encounter between God and His servant is as electrifying as the static electricity that often sparks around the top of Mt. Sinai. I remember one cold winter morning, having ascended to the summit of that same mountain, standing with three companions and suddenly realizing that every hair on our bodies was standing straight out. When we reached out to touch each other, sparks jumped from our fingertips. Even our clothes seemed lifted away from our skin, so powerful was the electrical charge between the low-hanging clouds and the great granite and flint mountain.

It must have been that way when Moses, his heart aflame with a fire that threatened to consume him unless God responded, cried out to his Lord.

Perhaps it was this consuming passion that impressed God. Perhaps it was the fact that Moses had removed himself from the people and, in silence, wanted to see the face of God for no other reason than to see the face of God. Whatever the reason,

God's response was one of total elation. It was as if He Himself had thrown all caution to the winds as He answered: "I will cause all my goodness to pass in front of you, and I will proclaim my name, the Lord, in your presence."

Then, realizing He was about to offer something to Moses that would literally consume him, which no man could comprehend, He backed off. "But," He said, "you cannot see my face, for no one may see me and live."

He then directed Moses to a place on the mountain. "There is a place near me where you may stand on a rock. When my glory passes by, I will put you in a cleft in the rock and cover you with my hand until I have passed by. Then I will remove my hand and you will see my back; but my face must not be seen" (cf. Exodus 33:12-23).

It was as close as any man in history would come to seeing the face of God, until God's Son, Jesus the Messiah, would appear to reveal Jehovah in all His glory. Of Jesus, the apostle Paul said, "For God was pleased to have all his fullness dwell in him," and, "For in Christ all the fullness of the Deity lives in bodily form" (Colossians 1:19; 2:9).

Moses returned from his encounter with God a man of few words. Yet something had happened inside him. His face literally glowed with the glory of God—a shine that was so great he had to actually wear a veil to keep from being conspicuous. The words he did speak, however, were words of great power.

Words rooted in the soil of God are words that have emerged from the silence and lead us back into that silence.

Silence, we have been told, is emptiness. But in our walk through the wilderness, as we close our door on the shouts of men, the clashing of ideas, the clamor of things, even the music of praise, we find that silence is not emptiness, but Fullness and Presence. Here we get a glimpse of the great mystery of God—the mystery of God's own speaking.

Out of the silence and darkness of the past, God spoke the Word and through this Word created heaven and earth. As it was in the past, so it shall be in the future. For when the final seal—the seventh seal—was broken in John's revelation of things to come, "there was silence in heaven for about half an hour." Only when that silence was complete, and God's awesome mystery fully comprehended, was the angel allowed to approach the golden altar before the throne with the spoken prayers of the saints. Only after the silence were the seven angels allowed, one at a time, to put the trumpets to their lips to sound the blast that heralded the advent of the establishment of God's eternal Kingdom. Words may be the instruments of this present world, but silence is the mystery of the future world, and heralds the presence of God (cf. Revelation 8).

Hours before sunrise, after that awesome, silent experience at the base of Mt. Sinai, our small group of men arose to begin the three-hour climb to the summit. Our desire was to climb the mountain the way God had told Moses to do it. "Be ready in the morning, and then come up on Mount Sinai. Present yourself to me there on top of the mountain" (Exodus 34:2).

It was 3 a.m., and in order to reach the top by dawn, we had to climb in the dark. The night before, I had arranged for a young Bedouin boy, no more than twelve years old, who knew the path, to guide us up in the pre-dawn hours.

We began our climb in the chilly darkness. Feeling our way over the rocks, we finally reached the ancient camel path to the summit. The stars were brilliant, and I soon realized, as my eyes adjusted to the dim light, that there was enough light for the climb if we moved slowly, deliberately toward the peak—still another 3,500 feet above us.

All the men had flashlights. They crowded close together, on each other's heels, as they stumbled upwards. Falling over rocks, bumping their shins, they called out to each other words of caution.

Something was wrong. Mt. Sinai should be climbed as Moses climbed it, in silence. I stopped our young guide and called the men around me on the path.

"Put your flashlights away," I said. "Now stand still for a few moments. You'll find you will soon develop a night sight that will allow you to see in the darkness with the aid of the stars."

Then I asked them to space themselves several hundred feet apart and begin the ascent again, one at a time, in total silence. "For most of you, this will be your only opportunity to climb the Mountain of God. Do not spoil the moment by talking about inane things. Be silent. Let God speak to you as you climb."

So we did, each man climbing at his own speed up the steep path. As our eyes grew accustomed to the starlight, the rocks and mountains began to take shape around us. We could see the steep precipices beside the trail, falling off hundreds of feet into the valleys below. But there was ample light to see the entire panorama of the Sinai as it spread out before us with each ascending step. High above us, its craggy peak rearing in awesome grandeur against the starlit sky, was the summit of Mt. Sinai. In the silence God began to speak to my heart, just as He has to all men who dare the risky walk of faith.

In the thin cold air I walked silently, the only noise the crunch of my feet on the rocks. With each step in the darkness, it seemed His Spirit touched another tender area of my life, bringing revelation and healing. My heart was consumed with joy. I paused, listening in the silence, looking out over the dark mountaintops of the entire southern peninsula. Moses had stood here, hearing this same voice, looking forward to the perfect revelation of God through His Son which I now looked back upon. I could almost feel the glory of God in the moment. I breathed deeply. Silently. And moved on up the path.

I was far ahead of the group, and at one place I rounded a dark bend in the trail and could see, stretched out below me on the winding path, the dim figures of the twelve men, fellow pilgrims, spaced along the trail far below. Then I saw something else. The last two men had grown discouraged. They had turned on their flashlights and were climbing by artificial light. Unlike the rest of us, their sight was limited to the small circle of light in front of them. They could not see what I saw— the heavens, the majestic mountain peaks, the saw-toothed ranges stretching out toward the eastern sky that was now turning a pale rose against the black, heralding the coming of the sun. All they could see was that small circle of yellow light in front of them. The others, although they were walking in darkness, could see the entire landscape, even though on occasion they stumbled over the small rocks before them.

I was sad. The two men with flashlights would reach the summit and enjoy the sunrise along with the rest of us. But they were missing the greater glory that came by climbing by starlight. With their conversation, although muted and whispered, they were drowning out the voice of God that spoke to all the others in a profound and personal way.

There is a time, it seems, in our walk through the wilderness, that we must risk walking in darkness and silence. It is at this time we must take our understanding and comprehension of things as they seem, fold it into our backpack and walk with only the hand of God guiding us.

That is the lesson of the silence in the wilderness.

XVII

Solitude

Then Moses entered the cloud as he went on up the mountain.
And he stayed on the mountain forty days and forty nights.
(Exodus 24:18)

There are times when a man needs his family and his friends around him—to comfort him, affirm him, correct him or heal him. But there are other times when each of us needs to be alone, totally withdrawn from all human voice or presence, separated from the world in solitude with God.

Whereas silence is passive, solitude is an act of seeking and finding that place of aloneness. Deep inside, all of us seem to know intuitively that until we withdraw from all we consider necessary to our comfort, we will not come face-to-face with God. It is that nagging truth that keeps driving me back into the desert. It is that same truth that has sustained me as I have walked through my own inner wilderness.

Only in times and places of solitude do men have genuine confrontation. Jacob was a family man, surrounded by wives, concubines, children, kinsmen, handmaids, warriors and workers. But there came a time in his life when he realized he could no longer hide from himself. Sending everyone ahead, he knelt one night beside the Brook Jabbok and entered into solitude. There ensued that night a great battle as Jacob wrestled with a heavenly being. As dawn approached and it was evident Jacob's stubbornness had not yielded, the angel started to leave. But Jacob, realizing he was fighting against something he desperately needed, cried out, "I will not let you go unless you bless me" (Genesis 32:26).

The blessing came in the form of a hip deformity. From that time on, Isaac's younger son walked with a limp. But his life, as well as his name, was changed. No longer was he called *Jacob*, the manipulator. Now he was called *Israel*—one who wrestled with God, and lost.

When our wrestling is alone, as with Jacob at the Brook Jabbok, we come to understand the real battles we face are not with others, but with self—and with God. Only then do we understand that the purpose of the wilderness is not to break us, but to soften us so we may be molded into the image of God's Son. For God does not want broken men, only men who are yielded.

For this reason, however, we fear solitude even as we fear silence. As soon as we are alone, without people to talk to, books to read, TV to watch or phone calls to make, an inner chaos opens in us, threatening to swallow us like ships caught in a giant whirlpool. Thus we do everything we can to keep from having to be alone. We create activity involving others, we spend long nights in bars, we latch onto unhealthy relationships or create situations that demand others come to us. We feign need or sickness or, using some kind of twisted reverse psychology, stalk away from people hoping someone will come running after us. "Do not leave me alone!" is the cry of every lonely heart. And "solitary confinement" is considered the worst of all punishments man can mete to man.

Yet Moses, Elijah, David and Jesus—and millions of others who have walked through the wilderness—discovered that solitude is not a curse but a blessing. It is not something to be feared but a treat to be desired.

Over and over we read that Moses went alone—into the desert, up a mountain, into his little "tent of meeting"—and there he met God. In solitude we become present to ourselves. There we can live, as Anne Morrow Lindbergh says, "like a child or a saint in the immediacy of here and now." In solitude every act is a desert oasis, standing apart from the burning sand of our pilgrimage. Cleared from the encumbrances of time and space, we relish each sense. Here in this wonderful oasis, we are free to drink the water, rest in the shade, taste the delicacy of each fruit and reflect on the meaning of God and self. Solitude does not pull us away from our fellow human beings, but instead makes real fellowship possible in the right time and the right place.

Thomas Merton, who spent the last years of his life as a hermit, said his contemplative solitude brought him into intimate contact with others. In his diary he wrote: "It is in deep solitude that I find the gentleness with which I can truly love my brothers. The more solitary I am, the more affection I have for them. It is pure affection and filled with reverence for the solitude of others."

Merton, of course, was right. It needs to be mentioned, however, that while solitude brings us into encounter with God, the lack of conflict with brothers and sisters, the absence of "rubbing," often presents a false image of true love—a love without confrontation.

Solitude, however, does not separate us from those we truly love, but brings us instead into deep communion with them—even though we may not see them for long periods of time. It teaches us to respect the solitude of others. We do not go crashing in every time we see someone alone, feeling we must provide company, for we realize that to do so might interrupt the deepest communion one can have—communion with God and with self.

Yet the mere thought of having to spend time alone is terrifying to most of us. To be sent into a wilderness is bad enough, but to be sent alone is more than we can bear. We seem to realize that when we are alone, we are forced to face ourselves—and to face God. We use outer distractions, therefore, to shield ourselves from the interior noises, and from the awesome voice of God. Thus it is not surprising most of us do not like to be alone, or when we are alone, fill the time with mind-occupying activities. The confrontation with our inner conflicts is too painful to endure.

Jesus, however, told us: "When you pray, go into your room, close the door and pray to your Father, who is unseen" (Matthew 6:6).

This concept of the "prayer closet" is the thing that keeps many of us from praying at all, or at least limits our prayers to those we utter in public. For we know that entering a private room and shutting the door does not mean we leave all our doubts, fears, guilts, memories, angers and insecurities behind. Indeed, it means we often bring them with us into our prayer closet where, since they have no room to swirl around us, they come crashing down on top of us, forcing us to face them.

It is for precisely this reason Jesus said we should often pray alone. How else can we get honest with ourselves? How else can we hear the voice of God?

Although the desert fathers were men of solitude, they were also hermits, and as a result became parasites upon others who had to feed and protect them. This is the primary reason they died out. There was no sustained effort at reproduction. Thus, while their experiences teach us much of the value of silence and solitude, only a few of the desert fathers are worthy to be singled out as models for others making their way through the wilderness.

One of these was Abbot Anthony. After working as a poor laborer in Egypt in the middle of the third century, Anthony withdrew into the desert, where he lived for twenty years in complete solitude. During that time his worldly shell was cracked and the abyss of iniquity opened to him. But because of his unconditional surrender to Jesus Christ, he emerged from the desert a changed man.

The fact that he emerged qualifies him as a model. Most hermits entered the desert to remain the rest of their lives. But Anthony felt the lessons learned in solitude should be shared with others. This made him a pilgrim as well as a hermit. Even though he returned to his hermitage in his old age, he first shared with others all he learned from his prior walk with God. During this time people flocked to him, recognizing spiritual wholeness and the ability to minister healing, comfort and direction for other sincere seekers. All this came as a result of his solitude. Returning to his cave in the Sinai, Anthony died in the year 356 A.D. at the age of 106.

The story of Anthony shows that solitude can become the crucible in which genuine transformation can take place. Moses had no time for God as long as he was active in the courts of Pharaoh in Egypt. Only when he was thrust into the furnace of the wilderness did he learn to listen. Alone, he discovered what his heart had so long been searching for in various companionships. He discovered God.

There are three basic things that keep us from solitude: insecurity, greed and anger. Like spiritual handcuffs, these forces manacle us to the presence of other people, preventing us from drawing aside long enough to face ourselves, or to come face-to-face with God.

Insecurity stems from not knowing who we are in Jesus Christ. Our poor self-image is fortified by the fear our sin will always dominate our lives. We refuse to believe the Word of God, which states clearly our position as sons and daughters of God. Since no one wants to continually face a sinner, we keep others around us so we can point out their sins and not have to face ourselves in solitude.

Our insecurity demands continual affirmation. Who am I? I am one who needs to be liked, needs to be praised, needs to be admired, needs to be touched. Or perhaps I need to be hated, need to be rejected, need to be held up as a poor example. Always there is fear lurking that we are failures, that if the onion of our life is peeled away, the inner core will be empty. So we refuse to get alone, afraid we might meet ourselves and not like who we meet.

Greed and anger are the sour fruit of our dependencies upon people, rather than our dependency upon God. Anger is that bitter response to the experience of being deprived of something. Depending always upon what others think of us, we react with anger when someone criticizes us. Likewise, if our dependency is on what we have rather than who we are, then when we cannot acquire what we want, greed takes over and we demand more. Insecurity, anger and greed are evil deputies chaining us to depend upon others for our identity, rather than allowing us the privilege of slipping away alone into the presence of God.

But when we enter the furnace of solitude, all that is burned from us. Without solitude, we remain victims of a society that forces us to look to others for meaning. Jesus entered the furnace of solitude immediately following His baptism. He was "led by the Spirit into the desert to be tempted by the devil" (Matthew 4:1). Like Moses, He was alone in that desert place for forty days and nights. In His case, His aloneness brought Him face-to-face, not with His Father but with His archenemy, the devil.

Three times He was tempted in the areas of Everyman's compulsions: insecurity, greed and anger. He was offered the kingdoms of this world; He was tempted to test God; He was tempted to turn stones into bread. In each case, Jesus answered out of personal security and a solid self-image. He knew who He was. When the lengthy time of solitude was over, He emerged "in the power of the Spirit" ready to begin His ministry of miracles.

Jesus, like Moses, found solitude to be a place of great struggle and great encounter. It was the place of struggle against the lies and accusations of false identity, and it brought an encounter with a holy God who loved Him enough not to make the way easy.

This struggle is often called the *agonia*. This is the classic struggle that every man must undergo to realize his full potential. It encompasses this eternal question: What is God trying to do in and through me by way of suffering?

In the New Testament, we find Jesus took this suffering and conquered it for us—not to prevent us from experiencing our own *agonia*, but as we carry our cross with Jesus to experience what Paul described as "the fellowship of sharing in his sufferings" (Philippians 3:10). It is this suffering that allows us to "attain to the resurrection from the dead" (Philippians 3:11), rising with Him to the full and perfect life He offers. As Augustine reminded us, "God's glory is man fully alive."

St. John of the Cross, the ancient mystic, described the *agonia* as "the dark night of the soul." Such suffering is not endured in the presence of others—only in solitude. It is in solitude we experience "the fellowship of sharing in his sufferings." If we attempt to do this in a group, then our fellowship invariably becomes horizontal rather than vertical, and we are able to rise only to the level of the group, not to the resurrection of Christ.

Yet it is this process of suffering alone, in solitude, that purifies us and produces fullness in our spirits accompanied by divine union between God and man. The dark night of solitude brings us to a hush, a stillness that enables the Holy Spirit to work His inner transformation. Like the oyster, which reacts to the grain of irritating sand by covering it with a hard substance, so the fellowship of sharing Christ's sufferings produces in us a pearl of great price, even though it may be evidenced only when men see us walking with a limp.

In our relationships with others, therefore, we must be careful not to remove a suffering God has placed on a man until the object of that suffering is complete—else we may deprive him of the pearl being formed in his soul.

In solitude the outer shell is pulled away and the true man emerges. Yet it is this true man most of us fear. We fear he may be another Moses, destined to spend his life in the wilderness—and we quickly force him back into the shell lest he grab us by the hand and take us with him. When we are alone, therefore, instead of facing the true man, we send in our servants of imagination and fantasy to clothe him in outlandish costumes. We send him out on imaginary journeys to exotic places, always to return and tickle our fancy with his exploits.

We picture him, not at all as he is but as we imagine him to be: wealthy, powerful, feared; or perhaps ugly, poor and dying. Seldom, if ever, do we allow him to emerge as the pearl he really is—a man of God fashioned by our own suffering and empowered by Christ to resurrection life. Therefore we often spend (or rather waste) our precious moments of solitude struggling with a never-ending effort to convince ourselves of our unrighteousness (or of our virtue), without daring to face ourselves—and God—naked and unadorned.

Looking at Moses, however, alone in his little tent of meeting, camping out on the Mountain of God, herding his sheep and goats through the empty wadis of the desert, we discover that it was this literal solitude that brought him face-to-face with the living God. Solitude is thus the place of purification and transformation, the place of struggle and encounter. It is the place where God remodels us in His own image and frees us from the images of self we all bring with us when we enter the wilderness.

While solitude should become a way of life, it should not lead to the extreme of constant aloneness. That was the mistake of the hermits. God wants us in families. He commands we should not forsake assembling ourselves together. Solitude, rather, is a matter of the heart—an inner disposition that allows us to enter our "prayer closet" at any moment, whether we are among others or not. It is Paul's concept of being in a state of constant prayer. It does not mean we must chase everyone from our lives or enter our cell and close the door forever. It does mean we will practice discipline as Jesus did when He, on regular occasions, stole away from His disciples and got alone with God.

Every pilgrim needs, as Moses did, a little "tent of meeting" where he can shut out all the world and commune with his Father "as a man speaks with his friend." But while the times of physical aloneness are desirable—even necessary—those who learn the real lesson of solitude realize it is found in the peaceful hearts of those who have entered into rest.

There is a vast difference, of course, between solitude and loneliness. While loneliness is inner emptiness, solitude is inner fulfillment. As loneliness is not healed by companionship, however, neither does solitude become beneficial simply because one is alone. The lonely person has no inner time or inner rest to wait and listen. He wants answers to his overpowering questions, solutions to his constant problems. But in true solitude, we learn we can be alone and not lonely. In solitude we come face-to-face with the One who satisfies all our needs. It's not that He necessarily answers all our questions or solves all our problems. But when we are alone with Him, they just don't seem important anymore.

So we enter solitude, as Moses entered the darkness of the Mountain of God, with no other motive than to be alone with the Father. We do not enter in order to return and share what we have learned. If we do this, we will spend our solitude time taking notes on how to apply truth to the lives of others. No, we enter solitude as an end in itself, not a means to the end of sharing.

We enter solitude to seek the face of God, to commune with Him as friend to friend, to let Him speak to us about the deep things in our hearts, and with an utter contentment to remain in solitude forever if He so wills. It is only then God sends us back down the mountain to the people below who are struggling with the concepts of community, to teach them that only as we come into His presence do we understand the true meaning of living in the presence of others.

XVIII

On Eagles' Wings

"You yourselves have seen what I did to Egypt, and how I carried you on eagles' wings and brought you to myself."

(Exodus 19:4)

Some years ago Episcopal Bishop James Pike, at that time an elderly man, ventured with his wife into the rugged Judean wilderness—a desert not unlike areas of the southern Sinai. Separated from his wife, he wandered hopelessly lost for several days. His body was found at the bottom of a wadi where he had stumbled, fallen and died.

To be lost in the desert without a guide means almost certain death. The guide not only shows us the way, but knows where we can find food, water and shade. Anyone who ventures into the wilderness needs a guide—one who has been this way before.

Moses was such a guide for the children of Israel. For forty years he had lived in the wilderness of Sinai. He knew every wadi, every spring, every well. He knew which canyons had no outlet. He knew the caves of the enemy Amalekites. He knew the ways of the Bedouin. Without him, the Exodus would never have taken place.

The Israelites were a nation of slaves when they left Egypt. For almost four centuries they had been taking orders from slavemasters. They were tenderfeet when it came to the rugged kind of survival procedures necessary to stay alive on their own. Even though they grumbled and complained about their guide, they knew they could not survive without him.

Moses, on the other hand, was aware of his own shortcomings. He knew his knowledge was limited, and that he would need help himself. Such was the case as the children of Israel turned north from Mt. Sinai and headed toward the Promised Land. Although Moses knew the paths of the Sinai, he also knew he would soon run out of knowledge as they made their way north into the Negev Desert. It was then that an interesting occurrence took place.

Jethro, Moses' father-in-law, had visited him shortly before he reached Mt. Sinai. He had come to return Moses' wife, Zipporah, to her husband. He doubtless stayed with the Israelites while they were camped at er Rakha near the base of the mountain. He listened with approval as Moses put his advice into effect, dividing the governmental duties among other leaders. Then, as the cloud began to move once again and the Israelites started northward toward Kadesh-Barnea, Jethro and his sons bade Moses farewell. It was time to return to their flocks in Midian.

At this point Moses realized he was about to enter unknown territory. He assumed the cloud would pause for only a short time at Kadesh-Barnea, and then the Israelites would move through the Negev Desert into Canaan. Moses had never been that far north before. He needed expert help. He needed a guide.

He turned to Hobab, his brother-in-law who was an expert guide and tracker, and asked him to leave his father and travel with the Israelites as their scout. At first Hobab refused. He realized the children of Israel were on the move and to move with them would mean he could not return to Midian. But Moses persisted. "Please do not leave us. You know where we should camp in the desert, and you can be our eyes. If you come with us, we will share with you whatever good things the Lord gives us" (Numbers 10:29-32).

It was a marvelous offer, to include a foreigner in the inheritance. It is similar to the implied offer Naomi later made to her Moabitess daughter-in-law Ruth, who had begged, "Where you go I will go, and where you stay I will stay. Your people will be my people and your God my God. Where you die I will die, and there I will be buried" (Ruth 1:16-17).

Hobab consented, and he joined his family with Moses and the children of Israel. Later in the book of Judges and in I Samuel, we find reference to Hobab and his family as ones who inherited a permanent dwelling in the Promised Land (cf. Judges 1:16; I Samuel 15:6, 27:10, 30:29).

It was an interesting commentary on Moses' leadership. Although the pillar of cloud was the real guide of Israel during their journey northward, yet Hobab's local knowledge was of great use in locating the springs and places of pasture. He became "the eyes" of Moses, as he used his vast knowledge of the terrain for the glory of God.

While the leader is always dependent upon God's guidance in his trek across the wilderness, there is also the need of human assistance—spiritual directors, so to speak. The people followed Moses, but Moses leaned heavily upon Hobab who, although he appears as a minor character in the vast drama of the Exodus, was nevertheless as indispensable to the great hero as those unknown Indian scouts who helped the American pioneers with their wagon trains as they crossed the uncharted wilderness of the Wild West. Moses depended upon the best means that human skill and knowledge could suggest, yet he followed the overall guidance of the Lord.

At the same time, unlike the wagonmasters of the West, Moses' one consuming passion was not so much to reach the Promised Land but to teach the people to depend upon God as he depended upon Him. Moses knew the time was coming when he would die. He wanted the people to know how to use every spiritual resource at their disposal as they moved forward—including how to rely upon human resources such as men like Hobab, whom God would send along to help them. A "super-spiritual" leader might have refused the help of Hobab, saying he needed nothing but the pillar of cloud. But Moses was wise to the ways of the wilderness—and the ways of God. He recognized that even those things that seem natural and humanistic can be tools placed in the hands of a leader by God Himself to make the task easier.

This was the reason Moses turned southeast along the Gulf

of Suez when he left Egypt. The most direct route from Egypt to Canaan was across the northern Sinai—the *Via Maris*, sometimes known as "the way of the Philistines." As modern archaeologists have confirmed, however, there were numerous Egyptian military garrisons stationed throughout the areas of the north along the sea—as well as the fierce Philistines or desert barbarians. "Lest the people repent when they see war, and return to Egypt," Moses led them south toward Mt. Sinai. He knew that during the intervening months, before they finally reached Canaan, he would need to show them how to meet and know the Chief Guide—the Spirit of God who had spoken to him from the burning bush.

Before turning south, Moses paused on the shore of the sea and sang a ballad, recalling all the events connected with the escape from Egypt.

> "I will sing to the Lord,
>   for he is highly exalted.
> The horse and its rider
>   he has hurled into the sea."
>
> (Exodus 15:1)

At the close of the song, his older sister, Miriam, picked up her tambourine and led the women of Israel in a dance of victory as they sang the refrain on the beach.

At the end of his life, Moses sang a second ballad. This one was much longer and more involved. Unlike the first song, it was not accompanied by dancing. In it, Moses emphasized that even though he had been the leader of Israel, it was God who had been their guide. Sensing he was about to die, he exhorted the people to "forget not" the Lord who had led them. In the ballad he compared the nation of Israel to a man lost in the wilderness without a guide.

> "In a desert land he found him,
>   in a barren and howling waste.
> He shielded him and cared for him;
>   he guarded him as the apple of his eye,
> like an eagle that stirs up its nest
>   and hovers over its young,

> that spreads its wings to catch them
>   and carries them on its pinions.
> The Lord alone led him;
>   no foreign god was with him."
>
> (Deuteronomy 32:10-12)

Moses' reference to the eagle was in obedience to the first words God had spoken to him 39 years before as he stood on the summit of Mt. Sinai. "This is what you are to say to the house of Jacob and what you are to tell the people of Israel: 'You yourselves have seen what I did to Egypt, and how I carried you on eagles' wings and brought you to myself'" (Exodus 19:3-4).

Now, at the end of his life, Moses reminded his forgetful flock of the certainty of God's guidance. He warned them not to put their trust in man, but in God alone. All these years in the desert had been for one reason alone—to teach them how to follow God's guidance.

The eagle literally "rides the winds" of the desert, soaring high above the storms with effortless control. The Hebrew word for wind is *ruach*. It describes the harsh *sharav* that howls out of the west and, whipping across the hot sand, roars through the deep wadis. It is often accompanied by flashing lightning and rumbling thunder. *Ruach* speaks of the hot air thermals that boil up from the blistering sand, causing twisting tornados and destructive hail. Yet upon such a wind the eagle soars, high above the desert, until peace is restored.

Veterans of the desert have seen the mother eagle carrying her young as God described it to Moses. This magnificent bird builds her nest on the face of the cliff. The nest is never completely at the top where it might be violated by preying creatures, but it hangs at a precarious spot on the side of the precipice.

The nest is large, constructed of branches laced together with the skill of a crocheted blanket. The mother then lines it with her own feathers to make it soft. Finally she lays her eggs.

Once the eggs are hatched, the mother eagle begins the seemingly endless chore of supplying food for the hungry eaglets. They grow at an amazing rate. Then one day a traumatic event takes place. The mother eagle comes to the nest, not to feed her babies but to push them out. Using her great head, she shoves one bird at a time to the edge of the nest. Suddenly, with wildly flapping wings and tiny shrieks, the eaglet is hurtling down the face of the cliff to the floor of the wadi far below.

Just before he hits the earth, the mother eagle swoops down and under him. By instinct, he clutches at the feathers on her back. With tiny talons he holds on for dear life as she flies upward and returns him to the nest. Then, just as quickly, she repeats the process. Over and over it is down with each eaglet, until the time comes when they no longer need her. They have learned to fly on their own.

Such is the task of the true guide—not just to take us by the hand and lead us, but to teach us how to find the way for ourselves.

Late one afternoon, as our small group was making its way up the long traditional Pilgrim's Path—the Naqb el Hawa—to er Rakha, the huge plain that stretches out at the base of Mt. Sinai, we paused to make camp. Before us, rising abruptly and starkly from the plain, was the dramatic apex of the Mountain of God. Catching the setting sun with hues of pink and purple, it was a breathtaking sight to see.

None of the twelve men in the group talked much as we approached the base of the mountain. Before long each of us had separated to find our own quiet place. I climbed onto a huge boulder, still warm from the day's blistering heat, and stretched out on my back.

The sun, a scarlet fireball, was slowly sinking behind the rugged mountains of the southern peninsula. No human sounds interrupted. There was no movement but soft wind, no sound but the awesome sound of silence. The sky stretched out above me in a thin, washed blue, the air as buoyant as a cleansing stream. To the east, the evening star appeared as the sun slid lower behind the surrounding mountains, throwing its slanting light and shadow across the deepening purple landscape. New colors were teased out of the stones: tans, grays, browns, streaks of iron red, copper green mixed with ancient hues of bronze and rust.

I let my eyes wander to the peaks of the towering mountains around me—gaunt, treeless, now caught in the descending shadows as the sun dropped below their jagged reaches. Sunsets in the Sinai are not reflected in the sky, but on the earth. The first touch of evening's chill reminded me it would soon become too uncomfortable to remain on my stone pedestal, apart from my companions. I was grateful, I realized, for our guide, who had brought us to this beautiful place.

There drifted through my mind, on a gentle current, a verse from the Psalms: "I lift up my eyes to the hills—where does my help come from? My help comes from the Lord, the Maker of heaven and earth. He will not let your foot slip—he who watches over you will not slumber. . . . The Lord is your shade at your right hand; the sun will not harm you by day, nor the moon by night" (Psalm 121:1-6).

I thought of Moses—and of all the other Moseses I have known—who have trekked the lonely wilderness of the soul and returned to lead others to the land of promise. I thought, too, of the unknown Hobabs, who have led the leaders. Each of us, leader or follower, has had such a person in our life, a spiritual guide who has shown us the way.

God, I thought, is no longer preparing a dwelling place for His people. Now He is preparing a people for His dwelling place. In the wilderness, He purifies and cleanses—and provides a guide to take us through.

As I slid off my rock to join my friends at the campfire who were sitting down to a small dinner eaten from mess kits, I thought of an inscription I once read on a rock in Wadi Taba, just south of the modern city of Elat, only a few miles from the place where the children of Israel finished their journey out of the wilderness to enter the Promised Land. It could very well have been the place where Moses sang his final song.

The inscription was carved by an ancient guide who had led his pilgrims across the burning wilderness to their destination near the Gulf of Aqaba. It says:

I am the guide who not only knows the way, but knows the wells.

The true guide knows both—the path and the place of provision.

There is an ancient legend that originated in the desert, although it has long since been modernized. It is the story of an old desert traveler who looked back on his life in a dream. In the dream, he saw his footprints as he walked across the sandy wilderness of life. As he retraced his steps, he saw for the first time that he had been accompanied by a guide, for there were two sets of tracks. The second set belonged to the Lord, who had walked with him throughout his life.

But there were places in his life, difficult places he could recognize, where the second set of footprints disappeared. Recognizing these places in life as the places where he had experienced his deepest adversity—places of grief, despair and hopelessness—he cried out to the Lord.

"Why," he questioned, "did You leave me to walk alone during those times? It was then I needed You most."

"You don't understand, My child," the Lord replied gently. "I did not leave you in the difficult times. The reason you see only one set of footprints is that during those times I was carrying you."

"You have seen how I carried you on eagles' wings and brought you to myself."

XIX

Covenant Love

*And they said to each other, "We should choose a leader and go
back to Egypt."*

(Numbers 14:4)

It is never God's intention to keep His children in the
wilderness any longer than necessary. It took only eleven
days for the Israelites to march from Sinai to Kadesh-Barnea.
Here God intended the people to regroup after their forced
march, feed their flocks, then go in and take the land He had
promised them.

But history records they grew fainthearted at the last minute. Fearful they could not do what God commanded, they
backed down. Surely it was the greatest disappointment in the
life of Moses.

It never entered Moses' mind that the Israelites would do
anything other than complete the march from Egypt to Sinai,
receive the Law, and then follow God straight into the Promised Land. The idea that he would have to spend an additional
forty years in the wilderness—having already served his time
of preparation—was foreign to him. No doubt he was already
planning the conquest of the new homeland and visualizing
how the government of God would be established.

But something happened after they reached Kadesh-Barnea, that sparse oasis in the northern Sinai that was within
literal sight of the Promised Land. Pausing there to regroup
his forces, Moses was approached by a delegation from the

people who said, "Don't you think it would be a good idea to send spies into the land before we move across the border?"

This was not part of God's original plan. God intended for the people to march forward, under the cloud of His anointing, and possess the land. They had already come more than 400 miles in fifteen months. Surely they had learned by now that God was faithful and could be trusted; that if He asked them to do anything, He would also provide the means to accomplish the task.

But instead of moving out with the morning's light to take the land, the people hesitated. It was the first step toward unbelief. Even though God seemed to permit the episode of sending out spies, the proposal did not originate with Him. Forty years later, when Moses was recounting all that took place, he reminded the people: "Then all of you came to me and said, 'Let us send men ahead to spy out the land for us and bring back a report . . .'" (Deuteronomy 1:22).

As in the case when the Israelites later demanded a king, God gave them what they asked for. Instead of acting in faith and believing God, they acted cautiously, fearing there might be giants in the land, walled cities and obstacles too great for them to overcome. Sure enough, there were. They received what they confessed, and their negative faith brought about their downfall.

Had not God promised them the land? Had He not proved faithful at every turn of their journey? Could they not trust His decision to go in at once and possess the land? Had He not said He would fight their battles for them? Why, then, this need to spy out the land? All they had to do was go up and possess the land. The command was simple: "See, the Lord your God has given you the land. Go up and take possession of it as the Lord, the God of your fathers, told you. Do not be afraid; do not be discouraged" (Deuteronomy 1:21).

Faith marches ahead when God speaks. But the Israelites "were not able to enter, because of their unbelief" (Hebrews 3:19).

It was spoken first in the murmur of caution from the people. Moses, unfortunately, listened. Instead of hearing faith, he heard unbelief.

Twelve spies were chosen, one from each tribe. Of these we

know the names of only two—Caleb, who "wholly followed the Lord," and Joshua, the "minister of Moses," whose name Moses had formerly changed from Hoshea (help) to Joshua (Jehovah is help).

The spies left the camp of Israel "at the time of the first ripe grapes"; that is, about the end of July. Skirting the army of the Canaanites who were encamped on the plain to the west of Kadesh, they entered the land and went all the way to the northern boundary of present-day Israel. Returning south, they passed through Hebron and the Valley of Eschol and explored the route that led into the Negev Desert by the western edge of the mountains. In one of these extensive valleys, they cut a gigantic cluster of grapes that was so heavy it took two men to carry it, slung on a staff over their shoulders. They also gathered pomegranates and figs and, after forty days' absence, reappeared in the camp of the Israelites at Kadesh-Barnea.

Despite their safe return, and the huge bounty they brought with them, only Joshua and Caleb gave a good report. The majority of the spies were negative. "[The land] does flow with milk and honey! Here is its fruit. But the people who live there are powerful, and the cities are fortified and very large. We even saw descendants of Anak [giants] there" (Numbers 13:27-28).

Caleb raised his voice. "We should go up and take possession of the land, for we can certainly do it."

But the other spies argued. "We can't attack those people; they are stronger than we are." Throughout the evening they went through the camp, poisoning the minds of the people, spreading fear and unbelief.

"The land we explored devours those living in it. . . ."

"All the people are of great size. . . ."

"We saw giants there. . . ."

"We seemed like grasshoppers in our own eyes, and we looked the same to them" (cf. Numbers 13:30-33).

People always love to hear a negative report, for the human heart loves to be deceived, loves to rebel against God. It is the nature of man to be fearful and to disobey God. Thus, when some voice of seeming authority speaks, or writes, the human heart listens.

The ten spies looked at the obstacles through the eyes of grasshoppers, but Joshua and Caleb looked at the difficulties through the eyes of God. The people, however, sided with the negative report. The obstacles were too many, the menaces too great. But in their decision, they made a fatal mistake. Unbelief never sees beyond the difficulties. It is always looking at walled cities and giants rather than at God. Faith looks at God; unbelief looks at the obstacles. Although faith never minimizes the dangers or the difficulties, it counts on God to overcome these things. The people, however, looked inward at themselves and saw themselves as grasshoppers. They tried to imagine how they looked through the eyes of the enemy and saw more grasshoppers. They failed to do the one thing Joshua and Caleb did—look at God.

That night, after the spies made their rounds through the camp distributing their poisonous reports, the people began to use worldly logic and reason. They said to one another, in effect: "We've made a mistake. If we stay here, our wives and children will be taken as plunder. It would be better for us to return to Egypt. We should choose a leader and go back to Egypt" (cf. Numbers 14:2-4).

It was the bitterest hour in Moses' life. After delivering them from the horrible slavery of Egypt, leading them supernaturally through the sea, seeing that all their needs were met, introducing them to the God of heaven and earth, interceding for them at Mt. Sinai when God would have destroyed the entire nation—indeed, offering his own life in exchange for theirs—and now bringing them to the very borders of the Promised Land, they had turned upon him.

Once before they had proposed to elect another leader to take them back to Egypt. But that was while Moses was away. This time the proposal was made to his face. It was as though a petition had been drawn up on his own parchment and placed on the pulpit as he stood to preach. The people whom he loved dearer than his own life, whose very existence was due to his intercession, had forgotten all he had done and were now declaring him an unfaithful leader. If he would not go with them back to Egypt, they would leave him alone in the desert with that small group who felt the same way he did.

The rejection was too much for Moses. He and Aaron, his

brother, fell on their faces before the entire assembly, too stunned to talk. Only Joshua and Caleb, still filled with faith and confidence, were able to speak. In anguish they tore their clothes and cried out, "Do not rebel against the Lord. Do not be afraid of the land. It will not devour us, we will devour it. The Lord is with us. Do not be afraid" (cf. Numbers 14:9).

Their resistance only made the people angrier. They picked up stones, prepared to rush the four men and stone them to death, when suddenly a tremendous light appeared over the tabernacle. God, whose presence had been only a shadow in the cloud over the camp, suddenly appeared visibly in a brilliant burst of His *shekinah* glory. The people were paralyzed over the appearance of Jehovah as His angry voice rumbled from the midst of the light of His glory: "How long will these people treat me with contempt? How long will they refuse to believe in me, in spite of all the miraculous signs I have performed among them?" (Numbers 14:11).

Then, speaking directly to Moses in a voice loud enough for the entire nation to hear, God said He was going to wipe them all out with a plague. He was going to destroy them, every last one of them, and start again with only Moses, Joshua and Caleb and their families.

There are certain times in every man's life when he makes decisions that change the entire course of his destiny. These are "hinge moments" on which swings the future. This was such a time in the life of Moses. God was offering him the inheritance He had promised earlier to Abraham. No longer would Moses have to contend with the fainthearted, the unfaithful, the grumblers, the unbelievers. In a single moment God would wipe out the entire nation of unbelievers and start afresh with Moses and those faithful men who stood with him.

"Accept it," said the spirit of self. "You've gone the second mile. You've turned the other cheek. This opportunity will never come again. Take your rest and enjoy all that is due you."

"No," said Moses' nobler self. "At stake is far more than my own self. As much as I yearn to rest, to no longer have to fight with these squabbling people, to become a second Abraham, I cannot do it. I have made vows to these people, and even if they do not want my love, I have no choice but to love them. If they cannot inherit the land, then I cannot do it either. Such is the price of covenant love."

Just ahead, only a few miles to the north, were the mountains of the Promised Land—a land flowing with milk and honey. It was all his, with God's blessing. He was within a day's march of paradise. It was the fruition of his life. All he had to do was turn his back on those who were refusing his love and move ahead. He glanced up at the mob surrounding him, some still holding the stones they would have used to kill him. There they were, standing like marble statues, immobilized by the mighty presence of the glory of God, their expressions frozen on their faces, unable to speak or move.

Were they worth giving up all he had earned over these forty years in the wilderness? Were they worth dying for? Across the years perhaps there echoed a word that would one day redeem not just the nation of Israel but the entire earth: "But God demonstrates his own love for us in this: While we were yet sinners, Christ died for us" (Romans 5:8).

"I cannot accept the offer," Moses whispered into the dust where he lay on his face before God. "I cannot go over and possess the land because they cannot go with me."

He knew, the moment he uttered the statement, what God's verdict would be: "Turn back tomorrow and set out toward the desert." In his spirit he knew his decision would mean he would never see the Promised Land. But he had no choice, if he were to remain true to his character. He could not take the rest he longed for at the expense of the people to whom he had committed himself, even though they had disowned him. So he turned away from the open gate to paradise and chose to suffer with the people in their affliction, rather than enjoy the pleasures of Canaan without them. It was a rugged path he chose to walk, a path that would mean another forty years in the wilderness and a lonely death on Mt. Nebo, still just out of reach of the Promised Land. But it was a decision that saved the nation of Israel and softened God's heart so that despite His heavy judgment, a remnant was saved to go in at a later time to take what God had promised.

In the last stanza of "The Road Not Taken," Robert Frost

poetically captures this human experience common to many of us walking through the wilderness:

> I shall be telling this with a sigh
> Somewhere ages and ages hence:
> Two roads diverged in a wood, and I—
> I took the one less traveled by,
> and that has made all the difference.

So Moses chose the road of covenant love, the lonely road. In doing so he chose the road that God's Son, many years later, would walk also—a road that, despite the pain of having to see His servant suffer in behalf of His people, brought immense pleasure to God.

God's judgment of Israel was devastating. "I have forgiven them, as you asked," He told Moses. "Nevertheless, as surely as I live and as surely as the glory of the Lord fills the whole earth, not one of the men who saw my glory and the miraculous signs I performed in Egypt and in the desert but who disobeyed me and tested me ten times—not one of them will ever see the land I promised on oath to their forefathers. No one who has treated me with contempt will ever see it. . . . In this desert your bodies will fall—every one of you twenty years old or more. . . . As for your children that you said would be taken as plunder, I will bring them in to enjoy the land you have rejected. . . . For forty years—one year for each of the forty days you explored the land—you will suffer for your sins and know what it is like to have me against you" (Numbers 14:20-23, 29-34).

The inheritance was lost. What was theirs yesterday was today taken away, all because of their unbelief, their unwillingness to trust God.

Then the most amazing thing took place. The Israelites, in an incredible bit of twisted spirituality, reasoned that the way to undo their fate was to do the opposite of what they had done the day before. If God was going to punish them (already the ten faithless spies who had spread their poison report through the camp had died overnight of a horrible disease for not possessing the land), then surely the way to gain God's favor was to reverse their decision and set out the next morning to take the land.

Vainly Moses tried to stop them. He pointed out that God's decision was final. Not only that, the Ark of the Covenant would not be going with them; it would stay with him. But the people reasoned that all they had to do to reverse God's decision was to reverse their actions of the day before. They failed to understand what Job said sometime later: God requires repentance not only of what we have done, but of who we are. In this case, their sin against God was not their failure to possess the land. Their sin lay in rebellion against God and against God's leader—Moses. By their determination to go up the next day to possess the land, they were simply exhibiting how deep their sin was, for again they were refusing to submit to God's will and once again choosing another captain to lead them.

The wrong of rebellion and unbelief is not righted by attempting the exact opposite. It is still the same spirit which prompted the one that influences the other. Obedience that is not of simple faith is of self-confidence and therefore merely another kind of unbelief. It is not jutted-jaw determination that conquers the enemy; it is the presence of the Lord.

"Do not go up, because the Lord is not with you," Moses warned them. "Because you have turned away from the Lord, he will not be with you and you will fall by the sword" (Numbers 14:42-43).

But they did not heed Moses and added the sin of presumption to their disobedience. They presumed to go into battle without the presence of the Lord, when they should have been content to bow their knee, take their medicine, and give humble thanks that God even spared their lives. The result was disastrous. Moses recounted the episode in Deuteronomy 1:43-44: "In your arrogance you marched up into the hill country. The Amorites who lived in those hills came out against you; they chased you like a swarm of bees and beat you down from Seir all the way to Hormah."

As a result of his decision to remain with his people, a decision of covenant love, Moses spent another forty years in the wilderness. But unselfishness always brings its own reward—both on the person and on those he chooses to bless.

Although Moses never became a second Abraham, no man in history so typified the Son of God as this old leader—"Just as the Son of Man did not come to be served, but to serve, and to give his life as a ransom for many" (Matthew 20:28).

At the end of his second forty years, the Lord spoke again to Moses. "You have made your way around this hill country long enough; now turn north" (Deuteronomy 2:3). Even then the way was tough. They had to retrace their steps south all the way to Elat to escape war with the king of Edom. Then there were battles with the Amorites as they came north through what is now the nation of Jordan. There was an encounter with Balak, king of Moab, and a strange experience with a prophet named Balaam. There were final battles with warring tribes from Transjordan; but by that time the new generation of young Israelis had become an efficient, disciplined army. No longer were they a bunch of straggling, grumbling, ragtag slaves. They were, under Joshua, a fearsome military machine, ready to capture the walled cities of Canaan.

Moses gave his young charges final instructions. "When you cross the Jordan into Canaan, drive out all the inhabitants of the land before you. Destroy all their carved images. . . . Take possession of the land and settle in it. . . . Distribute it according to your ancestral tribes" (Numbers 33:51-54). He then appointed one leader for each tribe, designated the boundaries of the new land, and turned his back on the Promised Land.

It is not Mt. Sinai, with its rumblings and thunders, that frightens us. It is the silence and loneliness of Mt. Nebo—the fear of being left behind. That is the reason we build around ourselves elaborate structures, why we title ourselves with names of importance and standing, why we rush to join organizations. It is bad enough to be forced into a desert where the sun bleaches, where the hot wind dries, where the burning sand purges us of all our old ways; but to be left alone, to be left behind, is more than we can stand.

Yet all roads home lead through the wilderness. Here God allows the circumstances to strip us of all our nice things, to reduce us to primitive states. Here we discover the meaninglessness of material possessions and make preparation for the final day when our bodies, which we hold so precious, shall be reduced to ashes that the spirit may be liberated to glory.

As the Israelites, their wilderness lessons learned, moved toward the east bank of the Jordan, Moses slowly climbed nearby Mt. Nebo, which gave him an overview of the entire western scene from the Dead Sea to the Mediterranean. Beyond Jordan lay the lush, green Jericho valley close by the sparkling waters of the Dead Sea. High above Jericho, catching the rays of the setting sun, were the golden hills where one day David would build a new Tabernacle, where one day a cross would be raised, where one day the King of Glory would appear.

He stood there alone, his white beard blowing in the gentle wind, the gnarled and scarred rod of God in his hand. He had been left behind, this old man, as the new generation moved forward to possess the land. Aaron and Miriam had been buried in the wilderness. Zipporah was buried beside them. His sons had taken their place in the emerging nation. He stood alone—with God.

To some the scene is sad, but I prefer to believe Moses had transcended the need to occupy Canaan. It was no longer important, this world of rocks and sand. His long walk with God since that time he whispered his vow of covenant love had convinced him the things of this earth were nothing compared to what is most permanent and satisfying. True rest, he had learned, is never found in material things—even in a land of promise—but only in an abiding relationship with the heavenly Father.

I believe Moses was able to look ahead across the years, and see that the tiny strip of land far below, framed by the Jordan on the east, the sea on the west and the Sinai to the south, would always be a place of war and conflict. The descendants of Abraham, divided into factions, would continue their battle for possession of the land. But for Moses, the land was no longer important. The disappointment of Kadesh-Barnea was far behind. He would let those willing to fight for an earthly home go across Jordan. But he would stay behind, for he had found something far more satisfying than a land of promise.

After eighty years in the wilderness, he no longer needed an earthly house; his heart was content with the courts of God.

So out of the disappointments of Kadesh-Barnea emerged a man with another vision, laying hold of that which the moth of change and the rust of time could not destroy or corrupt. And on Nebo's lofty peak, as far below the new breed of Israelis moved in to possess the land, the old warrior turned his back and, with the arm of God around his shoulder, entered into the joy of his Lord.

XX

Spiritual Setbacks

[Elijah] traveled forty days and forty nights until he reached Horeb, the mountain of God. There he went into a cave and spent the night.

(I Kings 19:8-9)

More than halfway up Mt. Sinai there is a large green hollow at the very center of the mountain. The Bedouin call such a high mountain hollow a *farsh*—a mountain oasis. This one, majestic in its suddenness to the climber, is known as Farsh Eliahu, "Elijah's Farsh." From here, for the first time, the climber can see the actual peak of Jebel Musa—the Mountain of God.

One never encounters the farsh expectedly. Although I have climbed the mountain many times, I am always surprised by its appearance on the path. There are five paths to the summit from the bottom of the mountain. All end at the farsh, and from this point on there is but one trail to the peak.

The first time I climbed Mt. Sinai, I ascended from the back side, climbing by starlight in the darkness of early morning. Walking along that narrow canyon in the moments just before dawn, a flush of red light beginning to filter through the valley below, suddenly I was walking into a world of deep rose color, warm and welcoming. Extending above me were the sheer red granite cliffs on the eastern side of Mt. Sinai.

Where just moments before all was in deep purple shadow, now the rose hue of dawn reflected off the towering cliff, filling the deep ravine below with incredible colors that flowed across the saw-toothed ridges like a liquid rainbow. At my feet, the steep precipice fell away almost a thousand feet, straight down to the craggy rocks below. Ahead of me was a narrow cut through the rock—a vertical ravine with high black walls on either side.

I entered and thought of the valley of the shadow of death. Then the warm rose of the dawn filtered into the cut with me. The light intensified as I rounded a bend in the narrow path— so narrow I could reach out with either hand and touch the sides of the canyon. Beneath my feet the coarse sand crunched, and suddenly a deep flush of red and gold suffused everything—the walls, the floor of the canyon, myself. Squeezing through the tiny opening at the other end, I walked into a burst of brilliant gold light as the rays of the dawn sun filled the area before me. There, laid out before my feet, was the farsh—its tall green trees, called cypress trees, standing in cool and refreshing contrast to the brilliant gold light reflecting off the sides of the mountain.

At other times I have come up the front face of the mountain from St. Catherine's Monastery in the valley below. More than 3,200 steps have been hewn from the side of the mountain by zealous and dedicated monks in the early years of the last millennium.

There was a monk in the sixth century by the name of Stephanos, who spent his lifetime building and guarding a stone arch over the path at a spot just before the trail breaks into Farsh Eliahu, halfway to the top. After he finished the gate, he sat beside it in the shade, taking confessions from ascending pilgrims. His task was to discern the purpose of pilgrims who wanted to ascend Mt. Sinai. Those he found spiritually unworthy were sent back down the mountain, for, he felt, only those who were pure of heart could ascend the Mountain of God. Those who were impure, he believed, would be killed by the confrontation. The archway, known as St. Stephen's Gate, is still there—the entrance, so to speak, to the farsh.

There is, in every wilderness, a quiet farsh—a place of life-changing encounter. It is always a serendipity, a marvelous, sudden and unexpected discovery. One moment you are toiling upward, driven by forces you don't understand. The next moment you emerge into a beautiful "place of quiet rest, near to the heart of God." While high above on the isolated peaks the wind howls, in the farsh there is only a gentle breeze, cool shade and still water. Here the pastures are green, the table is set before you, and you find a cup overflowing with the goodness and mercy of God.

It was at this farsh, seated on an overhanging rock that extended over the floor of the eastern valley thousands of feet below, that I began asking that question which plagues all spiritual men. I had spent the night under that huge cypress tree, waking at various times and seeing its awesome silhouette against the starlit sky. Before sunrise, just as the first hues of gray began turning to rose, I had crawled from my sleeping bag, pulled on an extra sweater and climbed up on a rocky overhang where I could see the dawn reflected against the peak of the Mountain of God.

Why, I pondered, do those of us who live in the Promised Land keep finding ourselves back in the wilderness?

Surely, it seems, having once tasted of the blessings of God, there should be no desire, no need, ever to return to wilderness wanderings. Is not our ultimate goal to enter Canaan? Once there, then, why do we continually find ourselves back in the desert—wandering, thirsting, discouraged and sometimes without hope?

As gradually as the dawning of the sun that October morning, I began to fathom the answers to these perplexing questions.

Part of the confusion may stem from our misunderstanding of the nature of the Promised Land. The wilderness, in many aspects, was an easier place to live than the Promised Land. Granted, it was a place of wandering, a place of hard teaching, a place of painful purification. But it was also a place of provision and protection. There was free food every morning. There was protection from the vipers. God was visible throughout the day and night in the pillar of cloud and the pillar of fire. There was never any doubt about which direction to move. Concerning their entire forty-year trek, God reminded the Israelites, "Your clothes did not wear out, nor did the sandals on your feet" (Deuteronomy 29:5).

Yet when the wilderness training was over and the people of God entered the Promised Land, everything changed.

What was it that was actually promised in this Promised Land? It was "a land with large, flourishing cities you did not build, houses filled with all kinds of good things you did not provide, wells you did not dig, and vineyards and olive groves you did not plant . . ." (Deuteronomy 6:10-11).

Nothing was handed them on a silver platter, however. While God did promise Joshua, who led the Israelites across the Jordan River into Canaan, "I will give you every place where you set your foot . . . I will never leave you nor forsake you," He was not talking about nirvana, which is the popular view of what the Promised Land should be. Nirvana is a Buddhist concept of a state of perfect blessedness achieved by the extinction of individuality, by the extinction of all desires and passions and by the absorption of the soul into the supreme spirit. Nirvana is eternal blah-ness.

God's plan for His people in the Promised Land is far greater than the extinction of all desires. In the Promised Land, desire and passion are heightened. Granted, that necessitates self-control. But God never takes away our desires and passions. Instead, He heightens them. Then He focuses them to be used and enjoyed inside the framework He has designed. Sexual pleasure is designed for culmination in marriage. The desire and consumption of fine food and wine is to be enjoyed inside the framework of temperance and self-control. In the wilderness every step was directed by the finger of God; but in the Promised Land, while men and women are free from the bondage of legalistic law, they are now governed by laws written on the heart. Such laws, I might add, demand far more discipline than those chiseled in stone.

Even though God promised Joshua all the land where he set his foot, it was still up to the people actually to "possess" the land. That was accomplished not by sitting and waiting, but by aggressive military campaigns. In the Promised Land the opposition was fierce. The cities (which had been promised the Israelites) were walled and occupied by giants. The fields (which had been prepared) not only had to be tilled, planted, weeded and harvested, but the farmers constantly had to fight off invading bands of marauders who waited until the crops were ready and then swept down to plunder and steal.

It is not easy, living in the Promised Land. In fact, to some degree it is simpler and easier to live in the wilderness—an argument brought up many times by those who wanted to return to the bondage of Egypt, and again by those who voted at Kadesh-Barnea not to go in and occupy the land.

Thus the question "Why do the people of God constantly find themselves returning to the wilderness?" needs to be examined closely. Perhaps the place of adversity is not the wilderness at all. Perhaps one has grown so accustomed to God's provision for wilderness people, he does not recognize that the hardships being encountered are unique to those who live in the Promised Land.

Despair, temptation, discouragement, conflict—these are not just wilderness situations. They are situations faced by those in the Promised Land as well. Training and growth continue even after we enter the Promised Land—and perhaps in heaven as well. Only in the Far Eastern concept of nirvana do conflicts cease and the individual is absorbed into the whole. The promise of Jehovah through His Son Jesus Christ is much, much greater than the promise of Buddha.

In God's Promised Land, even though there is conflict and pain, struggle and despair, it is for the purpose of growth and change. Instead of absorbing our spirits into His Spirit, He heightens our individuality by placing His Spirit within each of us. Thus we begin to experience the ultimate of being— individuality. With individuality comes the anxiety of having to make decisions and the pain of suffering the consequence of wrong decisions. God never intended man to become senseless. Rather, He intends us to use all our senses, to become in the highest degree sensual people. Such is the promise of the Promised Land.

Since there are moments when even Promised Land people flee (or are thrust back) into the wilderness, let's look at some examples.

The apostle John, after outliving all the rest of the original apostles who were martyred, spent the last years of his life exiled in the wilderness, alone on the isle of Patmos. What a horrible place to end his life on earth for the one whom Jesus loved! Yet here John received the final revelation of God. In his private wilderness he met God anew. Here he saw a "new heaven and a new earth . . . the Holy City, the new Jerusalem, coming down out of heaven from God, prepared as a bride beautifully dressed for her husband." Here he heard a voice from the throne of God saying, "Now the dwelling of God is with men, and he will live with them. . . . There will be no more death or mourning or crying or pain, for the old order of things has passed away" (Revelation 21:1-4).

John, in his wilderness, saw as no man has seen, beyond the Promised Land metaphor to Ultimate Reality. He saw, not shadows on the back of a cave, as the Greek philosopher Plato described, but the Reality of Light streaming from the throne.

The apostle Paul, fresh from his encounter with the living Christ on the road to Damascus and still enjoying the first blush of the walk in the Spirit, was suddenly dismissed from the church. Let down in a basket over the city wall, he was sent into the Arabian desert on a three-year sojourn. There, during those silent years, he was taught by God's Spirit in the heart of a spiritual and physical wilderness.

Yet on his return he was judged by his fellow Christians to be immature and unfit for the ministry. Once again he was forced out of the church. It was the ultimate in rejection for the former Pharisee. His wilderness continued for eleven years, until God spoke to Barnabas and told him to go to Tarsus and fetch Paul to help with the ministry in Antioch. The wilderness was over, but the persecution never ceased, even though Paul was in his "Promised Land."

Jesus, Luke tells us, fresh from His baptism experience in the Jordan River, was "led by the Spirit into the desert." There, for forty days, He fasted and was submitted to great temptations by the devil.

Surely all these men—even the Son of God Himself—must have asked why. Why, after experiencing the taste of the Promised Land, am I once again in the wilderness?

We can only speculate on the answer—for seldom has God revealed the full answer to the question *Why?*

Far more important than *Why?* is the question *What?* That was the question God asked the prophet Elijah following his two-day run into the Negev Desert. Elijah was fresh from his amazing victory at Mt. Carmel where God had answered his prayer and caused even the heathen to cry out, "The Lord, He is God!" Then, hearing the threat of Queen Jezebel to have him publicly executed, Elijah's mood swung from elation to despair. He fled south.

Arriving at Beersheba on the southern border of Israel, he discovered a city filled with idolatrous shrines and a people committed to heathen licentiousness. He knew such a place would not tolerate the presence of Jehovah's prophet, fresh from the execution of the priests of Baal. So, leaving his servant behind, he ran farther south into the Negev, across the wilderness of el Thei until he came to a place of exhaustion.

How does one describe this wilderness place where the prophet Elijah finally dropped, moaning and gasping under a rotem bush? "I have had enough, Lord," he vomited out. "Take my life; I am no better than my ancestors." Then he collapsed under the scrub bush—known characteristically as a broom tree—and fell into an exhausted sleep.

When he awoke, he discovered hot bread and a jar of water—left, perhaps, by some angel. It was then God asked His question—the one that still echoes across the desert to all of us feeling angry or sorry for ourselves in our wilderness situation: "Man of God, what are you doing here?" Frightened, unable to answer, Elijah scrambled from his hiding place and traveled south another forty days on foot until he came to the "mountain of God"—that magnetic place that had drawn Moses from the flocks of Jethro to hear a voice speaking from a burning bush. Now this prophet, coming not from the bondage of Egypt but fresh from having seen the hand of God in the land of promise, began his arduous ascent up the craggy sides of the awesome mountain.

And so Elijah, confused and weary, suddenly crested that point in his climb just above the spot where St. Stephen's Gate now arches over the stone path, and emerged abruptly into the farsh. It was in this spot that the man of God had a life-changing encounter with the God of man.

While the peak of Mt. Sinai is the soul of the mountain, Elijah's Farsh is the heart. Here in this magnificent place, still 1,500 feet below the summit, all the weariness and turmoil of those ascending the mountain disappears. The farsh is closed around with peaks, as though the mountain is purposely protecting its secret from the outside world. It is encountered as one usually encounters God—suddenly. One moment you are arduously toiling, step by agonizing step up the steep ascent of Sinai. Then, suddenly and without warning, you crest at a level point in the rough path and emerge into this beautiful high oasis.

The modern pilgrim who dares ascend Mt. Sinai and stops at this farsh sees before him a tiny white chapel and a stone grotto dug into the side of the mountain. In the middle of the patch of bright green grass is a well, and beside the well stands one of the world's most famous trees. It is a gigantic evergreen, known as a cypress tree. Its grace and height demand instant attention. The tree seems to have grown in spurts across the years. Each time it seems to have put forth more greenery. The trunk emerges from the green clusters, bare and devoid of life, to the next level where foliage again appears. It is as though there are three trees in one—a trinity of trees, so to speak. Next to it is a smaller cypress tree, surrounded by other smaller cypress trees and a still smaller crabapple tree.

The mountains rise up steeply in all directions. Although hermits once lived here, the area is now grazed daily by a flock of black goats herded by a sturdy Bedouin girl shepherd.

That chilly October morning, seated high on my rocky promontory overlooking both the eastern valley thousands of feet below as well as the farsh, I watched my companions crawl from their sleeping bags to begin the day. The three camels, which had carried our camping gear up the steep trail, had risen from their odd squatting positions where they spent the night and were grazing on the patches of green grass behind a low stone wall.

How deeply I am attracted to this quiet, awesome place, I thought. The words of Kebel's description came to mind:

> On Horeb, with Elijah let us lie,
> Where all around, on mountain, sand, and
>   sky
> God's chariot-wheels have left distinctest
>   trace.

There is a whole new world to be encountered in the farsh. It is a secret garden in the midst of the wilderness, a place of greenery, of smooth rock faces, of chapels and hermit's caves, a place of wonderful memory and rich tradition where cool water springs forth, green grass covers the harsh brown of the high desert floor, and from which point one can see the holiest of places—the summit of the Mountain of God.

For some the farsh is but a place of rest and refreshment before they resume the arduous climb to the peak. For others, like Elijah, it is a place where one can receive profound revelation and a quiet word to return to the land of promise. In the farsh God speaks not in the wind, earthquake and fire that echoes from the summit, but in the still, small voice of the heart.

In that place you are able to pause and realize that the wilderness is not always harsh and cruel. It can be soothing, a place of retreat and peaceful rest apart from the turmoil of those pushing upward in their own strength.

There is an ancient Bedouin legend: "Behind the el Thei is the desert of the lost." El Thei is that vast desert of powdery dunes that stretches along the northern half of the peninsula. The desert people, the nomadic Bedouin, fear it as a place of desolation. They prefer the rugged mountains and deep wadis of the southern Sinai.

Elijah had crossed el Thei on his flight to the Mountain of God. Now, resting in the farsh, he heard God telling him to return. The true wanderers, those who dwell in the wilderness, would never respond to such a voice. They fear el Thei and the desert of the lost. But to a man like Elijah, who had left the land of promise on his personal pilgrimage into the wilderness, the command to return to Canaan was welcome. Unlike the Bedouin who have no direction, no goal, who still simply wander through the wilderness, Elijah knew what lay beyond el Thei—not a desert of the lost but the land of promise. Refreshed and strengthened by his encounter with God, he returned once again to the conflict, walking strong in the strength of the Lord.

So we return to the original question God asked of Elijah: "Man of God, what are you doing here?"

God did not ask, "Why are you in the wilderness?" Indeed,

that is the question man asks so unceasingly of God. Rather, God asked, "Now that you are here, what are you going to do about it?"

It is this question that still confronts all of us who flee or are forced back into the wilderness from the safety of our Promised Land. Exhausted and weary, we finally get quiet enough in our flight to rest at the farsh. Again the question sounds: What are you doing when things go against you, when the Jezebels of this world threaten to destroy you? What are you doing when there is no money in your house; when a loved one dies; when the doctor says, "No hope"; when some trusted friend lets you down?

It is at this time that the man of God, the woman of God, should pause to regroup. Here are a few suggestions—things to do while resting at the farsh.

1. *Remember your past.* The farsh is a good place to stop and remember. An old saint once said, "When I grow weary of well-doing, when my faith sags and my spiritual heart faints, I remember. I go back to my former life before I became captive to God. I take a long walk up and down the street of my sinfulness. When I return, I am so full of thanksgiving to the God who saved me, so full of the mercy and grace of God, that my heart is once again singing and my feet dancing with joy."

2. *Reassess your position.* The farsh is a place to take spiritual inventory. It is a time to say with David: "Search me, O God, and know my heart; test me and know my anxious thoughts. See if there is any offensive way in me, and lead me in the way everlasting" (Psalm 139:23-24).

It is at the farsh that one begins to determine exactly who is behind the adversity. Is it God or Satan? The man of God, pausing even in exhaustion, will eventually hear the still, small voice reminding him of the everlasting love of God. He will also realize that when God puts His finger on something wrong in a man's life, it is because He loves him.

King Solomon warned his children: "My son, do not despise the Lord's discipline and do not resent his rebuke, because the Lord disciplines those he loves, as a father the son he delights in" (Proverbs 3:11-12).

On the other hand, Solomon said, "Stern discipline awaits him who leaves the path; he who hates correction will die" (Proverbs 15:10).

James told his readers, many of whom were suffering untold hardships, to "consider it pure joy" when they faced adversity, for they were learning perseverance. That perseverance, he told them, would bring them to spiritual maturity and completeness.

God always first warns His children in private. Only if they do not repent does He apply the rod in public.

3. *Recognize your friends.* How easy it is, when fleeing, to think yourself friendless. Once before Elijah had been alone in the wilderness. That time he was brooding over the sins of the nation at the Brook Kerith in the wilderness east of the Jordan River. While he was there, ravens—wild scavenger birds considered a national nuisance—brought him both bread and meat.

Now, again, we find Elijah exhausted in the desert. This time, however, he is running away. Fear controls him, and he is fleeing in panic.

Alone, fearful, desperate for help, he succumbs under a broom tree. While he is sleeping, someone stops by with a jug of water. Building a small fire of camel dung, this unknown "angel" bakes pita bread and leaves it for the prophet that he may eat and drink when he awakes.

God has His servants everywhere—in the most unlikely forms.

The wilderness is always a place of loneliness, while the Promised Land is a place of fellowship. The New Testament describes the church as a *koinonia*, a community, a fellowship. This same church is described as a family, with brothers and sisters.

That is why God never intends for His servants to remain in the wilderness. Even the lovely farsh is but a place to pause and be refreshed in order to return to the rigors and struggle of the Promised Land. In the farsh, God gently reminded Elijah he was part of a great family—with 7,000 brothers and sisters who had not bowed the knee to Baal.

The strategy of the devil is to keep people separated from

one another in a hell of isolation and independence, relating their lives to each other only superficially. While we are called on by God to sharpen our individualism, that is never to be done independently from other members of the family of God.

That's what the Promised Land is all about—individuals bound together. But it often takes a trip back into the wilderness in order to appreciate all that means.

In the third century Cyprian, who later became Bishop of Carthage and was martyred for his faith, wrote a letter from his own spiritual farsh. It was addressed to his old friend Donatus, explaining what had happened to him.

> This seems a cheerful world, Donatus, when I view it from this fair garden, under the shadow of these vines. But if I climbed to some great mountain and looked out over the wide lands, you know very well what I would see: brigands on the high roads; pirates on the seas; in the amphitheatres men murdered to please the applauding crowds; under all roofs misery and selfishness. It is really a bad world, Donatus, an incredibly bad world.
>
> Yet, in the midst of it, I have found a quiet and holy people. They have discovered a joy which is a thousand times better than any pleasure of this sinful life. They are despised and persecuted, but they care not. They have overcome the world. These people, Donatus, are the Christians, and I am one of them.

In every wilderness there is a farsh—a quiet place where one may hear God, receive fresh revelation, be refreshed and strengthened in order to return to the work in the Promised Land. It is there the true man of God, the true woman of God, is able to pray with the old French mystic: "Make me thy captive, Lord; then I shall be free."

Epilogue

On all my research trips into the Sinai, traveling each time with a small group of men, the last night in the desert has always been the most significant. It would be this time, usually camped in the sandstone regions north and east of Mt. Sinai, that we would sit around a campfire and reminisce over the events of our time together, expressing our camaraderie and experiencing the sadness that always comes when a beautiful event is ending.

It was on one of those last nights that the meaning of the "Law" and the nature of the "Law-giver"—which is what Sinai is all about—became evident to me.

Like the other groups in years past, this particular group of thirteen men had never met one another prior to our gathering in New York to fly to Israel. On that evening, however, nearly three weeks before, we had prayed together in a secluded part of the airport waiting area, asking God to let us, for the next several weeks, become "the church in the Sinai."

None of us fully understood what that meant, but we all sensed it meant we would do more than climb mountains and camp out in the desert. We sensed it would mean entering into a relationship with each other, a relationship of love and honesty. What we did not anticipate was the pain we would experience as we arrived at that place of transparency.

Our two Israeli guides, both tough young soldiers who loved the Sinai, became part of our experiment. Although they were much younger than the men on the trip, they immediately became part of our "church." Interestingly enough, although this group of American business and professional men—doctors, engineers, lawyers and one minister—were all accustomed to giving orders, they all readily submitted to the authority of our Jewish guides.

Early in the trip, as we left Israel to make our way into the Sinai, our guides outlined some basic principles. One of these mandates was: "We don't take anything into the desert and leave it there." That meant all trash, even orange peelings, would be collected and returned to Israel. The Jews were determined to leave the desert in its original, unspoiled state.

The other mandate was: "We don't take anything out of the desert which we find there."

This was hard on several of the men who had come with anticipation of adding to their rock collections. As an exception to this rule, the guides agreed that if we checked with them first they might allow us to remove a piece of turquoise or perhaps one of the beautiful crystals that are sometimes found in the vicinity of St. Catherine's Monastery.

The next-to-last night we camped on the southern seashore along the Gulf of Aqaba near the Jewish community of Ofira. We spent the night on the beach. That evening, as the tide ebbed, several of us walked out on top of the coral reef that was now exposed. We had our flashlights, examining the beautiful shells and creatures left in the little tidal pools.

When we returned to our camp to make ready for bed, the Methodist minister who was in our group pulled me aside. "I feel ill," he said, holding his chest. "Before we go to sleep would you gather the 'church' and pray for me?"

We did just that. I asked the minister to sit on a rock in the middle of a small circle while the other men stood around touching him gently with their hands in a time of prayer. Our two Israeli guides, although they did not participate, watched respectfully from a distance as the church met in prayer.

The next night was our last night in the Sinai. Instead of going inland we had driven north along the coast to camp again on the beach, this time near Nuweiba. Again we built a campfire on the beach. This time we sat and shared all the things we had experienced together—not knowing that the experience we were about to have would give new meaning to our spiritual understanding of life and relationships.

As we finished our time of sharing and were separating to go to our sleeping bags, which were spread up and down the beach, the minister again pulled me aside. "My sickness is much worse," he said.

I looked at him. He was in obvious pain. "Have you talked to our doctor?" I asked.

"I don't need a doctor. I need a priest."

"I don't understand," I replied.

"I am sick because I have sinned. Our guide told us not to take anything out of the desert. Last night on the beach I found a beautiful seashell—a big one the size of a man's head. I stuffed it into my duffle bag. The moment I did I began having chest pains. They have gotten much worse, and I'm afraid I'll die here in the desert if I do not make things right with God."

"Why don't you just throw the shell back into the sea?"

"That won't do any good. I deliberately broke one of the laws. I've got to go to our guide and confess. I want you to go with me."

I dreaded the confrontation. We had been hoping to impress our guides by our Christian character; now the minister in our group had sinned and needed to make confession. I kept remembering the story of Joshua and Achan in the Bible. God had told the troops of Joshua that when they conquered the city of Jericho they were not to take any loot. But a man by the name of Achan had disobeyed God. He had stolen gold and silver items from the captured city. As a result, the next time the Israelites went into battle at Ai, they were defeated. Joshua discovered Achan's sin and had him stoned to death. Only then were the Israelites victorious in battle.

I went with the minister while he talked to the guide who was in charge. He also handed over the purloined seashell—a beautiful pronged shell of many colors. The guide was polite, and even listened to the minister's story of Joshua and Achan, although I suspected he didn't know who either man was. When it was all over the muscular young man, sitting on the stump of a palm tree near the back of our truck, said, "It seems to me you need to tell this story to your church."

I looked at the minister. He swallowed hard but nodded in agreement.

A few minutes later I had rounded up the men and we were back at the campfire.

I related all that had happened. Then I pointed to the minister who was sitting, head down, as part of the circle of men around the fire. "What should the church do with a man like this? He is a thief who has broken covenant with the church. He has been rebellious against authority. He has lied and tried to get away with his sin. Now, however, he has come and confessed. What should the church do with him?"

No one spoke. As I looked around the ring of men—desert comrades seated on the sand with the reflection of the small campfire flickering on their faces—I saw every man had his head bowed in shame.

"Since no one has an answer, I'll ask our Jewish guide what he thinks we should do with this thief who has broken the command of the most high God."

I turned to our two guides and singled out the one to whom the minister had confessed. "Amir, what should the church do with this thief who has stolen this seashell?"

Sensing the seriousness of the situation, the young Israeli stood to his feet. "It seems you have several options. For one, you could ask him to do penance."

"That is the Catholic position," I said.

"Or you could cast him out of the camp."

"That is the evangelical position."

"But it seems you can't do anything unless you know his heart. Did he really mean it when he repented and gave the shell back?"

I saw all the heads in the group come up from their chin-to-chest position. They began to nod in agreement. Yes, if the law is not judged by the condition of the heart, then it is nothing more than a rule to be kept rather than a guide to be lived.

"That settles it," I said. "We all agree our brother has genuinely repented. He says the pains in his chest have disappeared—indicating God's touch on his life. That closes the matter."

"Not quite." It was the medical doctor in our group who had spoken.

"What do you mean?"

"Well, I've got a seashell in my bag also."

Another man raised his hand sheepishly. "I don't have any seashells, but I have a bunch of rocks I've been collecting."

We went around the circle of men. Everyone in the group had stolen something out of the desert. They had squirreled the rocks and shells away in their bags, stuffed them into their extra shoes with the hope of smuggling them past our guides and taking them back home as souvenirs. The entire church was a den of thieves.

As we discussed it we found there was some confusion about the guidelines. One of the guides had said it was all right to take a few small stones or shells. The other had said flatly, "Take nothing unless you check with me." The church had received conflicting direction from two authorities. The men were not thieves. They just didn't understand the law.

I couldn't help but smile. On the final night of our pilgrimage, the Church of the Sinai had been born.

Then another interesting thing happened: human nature took over. Instead of dealing with what our Jewish guide had called "the matter of the heart," someone said, "Why don't we bring all the shells and rocks out and lay them here on the sand? Then we can measure them. We'll keep the little ones and leave the big ones in the desert."

The other men agreed enthusiastically. "That will settle the matter," one man, an attorney, said. "We can tell what is right and wrong by the size of the shells."

The shift of spiritual direction was terrifying. One moment we were a body of men, confused over direction but willing to judge only on the condition of a man's heart; the next we were a group of legalists ready to draw up rules and regulations and judge sin by the size of the seashell.

"What is a big shell and what is a little shell?" I asked.

The men looked at me. They hadn't thought of that. We had no absolute standard; and size, like sin, is often relative.

"We'll have to draw a line someplace," one of the men said. "Why don't we say anything over one inch in diameter is to be left behind?"

I looked over at our two Jewish guides. They were grinning. It was Amir who finally spoke, laughing: "Now you sound like my ancestors. It's not enough for God to give a law that speaks to the heart; you have to write a Talmud to explain the law. Why don't you go all the way and set up a Sanhedrin to decide which shells are big and which are little?"

Even though the campfire was dying, it was easy to see that every man's face had turned red. What had started as a matter of the heart had quickly become legalistic and mechanical. Rather than looking on the inward parts, we were looking on the size of the seashells. We finally decided the matter was too weighty for us to determine. By common consent we resolved that each man would have to decide for himself, and leave the final judgment in the hands of God.

I suspect if mankind is going to survive, it will not be because we have gotten rid of the fellows who have stolen the big shells while keeping the fellows who have stolen only little shells. Nor are we going to survive by expanding on God's law (which is written on the hearts of His children) and setting up even more rules of things we can and cannot do.

We will not survive because we believe the same way, nor because we behave the same way. We will survive as God's people only as we are filled with God's Spirit, looking upon each man's heart as God looks.

That is the lesson of the wilderness.

That is the purpose of the law.

That is the heart of God.